PRACTICING WISDOM

→ 28 - Confuted
school of B that believes in atomistic world

PRACTICING WISDOM

The Perfection of Shantideva's Bodhisattva Way

HIS HOLINESS THE DALAI LAMA

Translated and edited by Geshe Thupten Jinpa

Wisdom Publications • Boston

Wisdom Publications, Inc.
199 Elm Street
Somerville MA 02144 USA
www.wisdompubs.org

Library of Congress Cataloging-in-Publication Data
Bstan-'dzin-rgya-mtsho, Dalai Lama XIV, 1935–
Practicing wisdom : the perfection of Shantideva's Bodhisattva way / Dalai Lama ; translated and edited by Thupten Jinpa.
p. cm.
Includes bibliographical references and index.
ISBN 0-86171-182-3 (pbk. : alk. paper)
1. Sāntideva, 7th cent. Bodhicaryāvatāra 2. Mahayana Buddhism—Doctrines. I. Title: Perfection of Shantideva's Bodhisattva way. II. Thupten Jinpa. III. Title.
BQ3147.B777 2004
294.3'85--DC22

2004021413

ISBN 0-86171-182-3

First printing.
09 08 07 06 05
5 4 3 2 1

Cover design by Rick Snizik. Interior design by DcDesign. Set in Granjon 12/14.5 pt.

The translation of the verses from Shantideva's *Bodhicharyavatara* is adapted with kind permission from *The Way of the Bodhisattva,* translated by the Padmakara Translation Group (Boston: Shambhala Publications, 1997).

Wisdom Publications' books are printed on acid-free paper and meet the guidelines for permanence and durability set by the Council of Library Resources.

Printed in Canada

CONTENTS

Publisher's Acknowledgment

The publisher gratefully acknowledges the kind help of Richard Gere in sponsoring the publication of this book.

EDITOR'S PREFACE

The ninth chapter of Shantideva's *The Way of the Bodhisattva,* which is the basis of His Holiness the Dalai Lama's teachings presented here in this volume, begins with the statement that it is for the sake of cultivating wisdom that the Buddha taught all the various aspects of the teachings. This seemingly simple assertion captures a profound insight that lies at the heart of Buddha's spiritual message. Unlike many of his spiritual peers, the Buddha argued that it is not through ascetic physical penance, through complicated religious rituals, nor through prayers that one attains highest spiritual awakening. It is through the disciplined taming of one's mind. Furthermore, since our bondage to a perpetual cycle of unenlightened existence is rooted in a fundamental ignorance of the very nature of our own existence, the cultivation of a deep understanding of the nature of our existence must constitute a central element of this spiritual discipline. Hence the emphasis on the cultivation of wisdom.

It is no exaggeration to assert that Shantideva's *The Way of the Bodhisattva (Bodhicharyavatara)* is one of the most important spiritual and philosophical texts of Mahayana Buddhism. Written in the eighth century C.E., this short work of just under a thousand stanzas soon became a classic on the topic of a bodhisattva's long journey to the full awakening of buddhahood. In contrast to *Compendium of the Perfections,* another classical Mahayana Buddhist work similarly written in verse and attributed to Aryashura (ca. fourth century C.E.),[1] Shantideva's text is not explicitly structured according to the well-known Mahayana framework of the six perfections. Although there are chapters (chapters 5–9) dedicated to each of the last four of the perfections—forbearance, joyous effort, meditation, and wisdom—the first four chapters deal with various aspects of the endeavor of generating the awakening mind *(bodhichitta),* while the final chapter (chapter 10) presents a series of deeply moving altruistic aspirations of the bodhisattva.

Shantideva's classic was first translated into Tibetan in the ninth century from a Kashmiri redaction. It was later revised by Lotsawa Rinchen Sangpo on the basis of a careful comparison with a central Indian edition of the root text and related commentaries; it was once again critically revised in the twelfth century by the famous Tibetan translator Ngok Loden Sherap. Thanks primarily to the early teachers of the Tibetan Kadam tradition, including its founding fathers—the Indian Bengali master Atisha and his principal student Dromtönpa, who regularly cited poignant stanzas from Shantideva's classic in their own teachings—*The Way of the Bodhisattva* came to enjoy tremendous popularity within Tibetan Buddhist circles. Alongside Nagarjuna's *Precious Garland*[2] and Asanga's *Bodhisattva Levels,*[3] Shantideva's text became a "root text" for the Tibetan tradition of *lojong,* mind training, where the central objective is the cardinally important spiritual endeavor of cultivating the awakening mind—the altruistic aspiration to attain buddhahood for the benefit of all beings—and enacting this altruistic principle in day-to-day life. The next eight to nine hundred years saw a tremendous increase in both the popularity and influence of this short work in all the major lineages of Tibetan Buddhism, attracting substantive commentaries from such great Tibetan teachers as the Sakya hierarch Sönam Tsemo, the lojong master Ngülchu Thokme Sangpo, the great Geluk author Gyaltsap Je, the Kagyü teacher and noted historian Pawo Tsuklak Trengwa, as well as the well-known Nyingma master Dza Paltrül.

The influence of this Buddhist text on the thought of the present Dalai Lama is unmistakable. Not only does he cite most liberally from it during his numerous public discourses on Buddhism, even in his engagement with the wider non-Buddhist audience the Dalai Lama shares his enthusiasm for Shantideva's *The Way of the Bodhisattva*. In fact, he cites the following stanza from Shantideva as his greatest source of spiritual inspiration and strength.

> For as long as space remains,
> For as long as sentient beings remain,
> Until then, may I too remain
> And dispel the miseries of the world.

Perhaps part of the reason for the great popularity of this classical Indian Buddhist work in Tibet lies in the beauty of its poetry. Most of the time the author writes in the first-person voice, with the elements of the various practices of the aspiring bodhisattva as a series of personal reflections. Many of his lines convey a powerful sense of immediacy, and their poignancy for a spiritual aspirant remains starkly evident.

Like many young Tibetan monks, I had the privilege of memorizing the text in my early teens and thus had the honor to recite the entire work from heart many times, often in the comparatively cool nights of southern India where my monastery was based. To this day, I can fondly recall the joy with which I went through the process of memorizing this text while working in the corn fields of the Tibetan resettlement camp to which my small monastery belonged in the 1970s. In the Tibetan edition, the stanzas are written in perfectly metered verse with a language that can rival any original Tibetan poetic work, easily lending itself to memorization and recitation.

This said, the ninth chapter of Shantideva's classic, the basis of our book, is a highly sophisticated and complex philosophical treatise. Shantideva opens the chapter with the following lines:

All of these elements of practice
The Buddha taught for the sake of wisdom.
So those who wish to pacify suffering
Must generate [the perfection of] wisdom.

With this statement underscoring the cardinal importance of cultivating wisdom, Shantideva sets out to systematically present what he understands to be the core of the Buddha's insight into the ultimate nature of reality. Being a proponent of the Middle Way school of Buddhism, for him the ultimate nature of reality is the emptiness of intrinsic existence of all factors of existence. In other words, the cultivation of wisdom entails the cultivation of the understanding of emptiness at its deepest level. Shantideva's presentation of the practice of cultivating wisdom can be broadly divided into the following three main sections: (1) presentation of the nature and characteristics of the two truths, (2) the need to realize emptiness even by those who aspire to attain mere freedom from cyclic existence, and (3) extensive presentation of the various reasonings establishing the truth of emptiness.

In part 1, in addition to defining his understanding of the nature of the two truths—the ultimate truth and the conventional truth—Shantideva presents a sustained critique of the philosophical standpoints of the Buddhist realists and idealists, with special emphasis on the views of the fellow Mahayana school, the Mind-Only. In part 2, as part of his overall argument for the necessity of the wisdom of emptiness even for the attainment of freedom from cyclic existence, Shantideva presents a systematic validation of the authenticity of the Mahayana teachings, including the validity of its scriptures. In doing so, he is following in the footsteps of some of his illustrious predecessors, such as Nagarjuna, Asanga, and Bhavaviveka, who too dedicated substantive writings toward the goal of establishing the validity of the Mahayana path. In the final part, Shantideva presents the various forms of reasoning, such as the famous reasoning of dependent origination, to establish the truth of emptiness as embodied in the Buddha's teaching on the selflessness of persons and the selflessness of phenomena. In the course of this, the author presents a wide-ranging critique of the various non-Buddhist Indian tenets, such as their postulation of the theory of *atman,* or eternal self, Samkya's theory of primal substance as the substratum of reality, Shaiva's assertion of the origination of things by means of divine creation, Vaisheshika's theory of indivisible atoms, the Materialist Charvaka's theory of accidental origination, and so on. The actual presentation of the meditation on the selflessness of phenomena or factors of existence is given in terms of the well-known formula of the four foundations of mindfulness—mindfulness of the body, of sensations, of the mind, and of mental objects. The chapter concludes with a moving exhortation to cultivate the wisdom of emptiness by relating wisdom to boundless great compassion for all beings.

His Holiness the Dalai Lama has given teachings on Shantideva's text, including the difficult ninth chapter, on numerous occasions, and some of these have already been published in contemporary languages.[4] What is unique about our present volume is that the Dalai Lama grounds his exposition of the ninth chapter as presented here on two interesting nineteenth-century Tibetan commentaries, each representing the perspectives of an important Tibetan Buddhist tradition. Khenpo Künsang Palden's commentary entitled *Sacred Words of My Teacher Manjushri* presents the perspective of the Nyingma lineage, while Minyak Künsang Sönam's commentary *Brilliant Lamp Illuminating the Suchness of Profound Dependent Origination* presents the perspective of the Geluk school.[5] Both authors were important students of the great Nyingma teacher Dza Paltrül, who was highly instrumental in revitalizing the study and practice of *The Way of the Bodhisattva,* especially within the Nyingma tradition. Both were active participants in the movement of nonsectarianism *(rimé)* that began in some parts of Tibet in the early nineteenth century.

The Dalai Lama not only provides a detailed stanza-by-stanza exposition of this crucial chapter of Shantideva's work, which has effectively become a philosophical classic in its own right, but he also intersperses his commentary with deep personal reflections on the practice of the Buddhist path. This latter dimension of the Dalai Lama's discourse was originally given as preliminary comments at beginning of every session when the teachings on which this book is based took place in France. We have separated these reflections from the actual commentary under the subheading of "Practicing Wisdom" so that the reader can follow the exposition of the root text more clearly. In juxtaposing the two commentaries while presenting his own personal understanding of Shantideva's root text, the Dalai Lama provides to the modern reader a richly textured experience of deep engagement with one of the most important religious and philosophical works of Mahayana Buddhism.

One consequence of the Dalai Lama's interweaving of two different commentaries reflecting the perspectives of the two important Tibetan traditions is to bring to the fore a highly creative debate that took place toward the end of the nineteenth century in Tibet. This began with the publication of a short exposition of the ninth chapter by the influential Nyingma thinker Ju Mipham Namgyal Gyatso, whose work attracted substantive critiques from several noted Geluk authors, including the well-known Drakkar Lobsang Palden, who was also a participant in the nonsectarian movement. As to the details of what are the key points of divergence between the readings of the chapter by these two Tibetan lineages, I will leave this to the reader to discern from the Dalai Lama's exposition presented in great clarity in this volume. To bring the philosophical reflections back to the basic framework of spiritual practice, many of the Dalai Lama's teachings conclude with a guided contemplative meditation on the key elements of the philosophical and spiritual reflections presented in the ninth chapter.

This book is based on His Holiness the Dalai Lama's weeklong discourse at Vajra Yogini Institute in Lavaur, France, in 1993, which was delivered at the invitation of an association of Tibetan Buddhist centers in France. The teachings were given as a sequel to an earlier weeklong discourse on the first seven chapters of Shantideva's *The Way of the Bodhisattva,* which took place in Dordogne, France.[6] With so many attendees coming from different parts of Europe, the teachings were translated into all major European languages, including English, French, German, Spanish, and Italian. In addition to being a serious weeklong Buddhist teaching retreat, it was also a wonderfully festive occasion with fellow Buddhist practitioners connecting or reconnecting with each other and sharing their personal understanding and experiences. As on numerous occasions, here too I had the honor of interpreting His Holiness' teachings into English.

Numerous individuals have helped to successfully produce the transcripts of His Holiness' teachings into the present book. Patrick Lambelet did the initial transcription; Samantha Kent entered the extensive editorial changes I made in the course of editing the transcripts; Gary Mutton did further editorial work that helped make the English much more readable; Dechen Rochard provided valuable feedback on numerous passages. To all of them, I would like to express my deep appreciation and thanks. Not least of all, I would like to thank Timothy McNeill of Wisdom Publications for insisting that I personally edit the transcripts of the teaching for publication, and, of course, my longtime editor at Wisdom, David Kittelstrom, for his incisive editorial comments at numerous stages of the editing process. For his continuously reining in my attention to the project throughout the several years it took for us to bring this most valuable series of His Holiness' teachings on Buddhist philosophy and practice into publication, I owe deep personal gratitude.

Thupten Jinpa
Montreal, 2004

1. INTRODUCTION

Developing Pure Motivation

Throughout this book, on my part as teacher, I have tried to develop as pure a motivation as possible to benefit you, the reader. Likewise, on your part, it is important to approach these teachings with a good heart and good motivation.

For those readers who are practicing Buddhists, and who take attainment of full enlightenment as their ultimate spiritual aspiration, it is also important for you to maintain the goal of becoming a good human being and warm-hearted person. With this aim you can ensure that your efforts here are beneficial, and will help you to accumulate merit and create positive energy around you. As you prepare to read this teaching, you should first take refuge in the Three Jewels and reaffirm your generation of the altruistic mind, aspiring to attain full enlightenment for the benefit of all beings. Without taking refuge in the Three Jewels, your practice does not become a Buddhist practice. And without generation of the altruistic aspiration to become enlightened for the sake of all sentient beings, your activities do not become that of a Mahayana Buddhist.

Some readers, no doubt, are not practicing Buddhists, but will nevertheless have a serious interest in the Buddhist teaching. Some readers will be from other religious backgrounds, such as Christianity, and will have an interest in certain aspects of Buddhist techniques and methods for spiritual transformation. For the readers who are not practicing Buddhists, you also can generate a good heart and good motivation as you prepare yourself to read these teachings; and if you find certain techniques and methods that you are able to adopt and incorporate into your own spiritual life, please do. If, on the other hand, you do not find any such helpful methods, you can of course simply put the book aside.

As for myself, I am just a simple Buddhist monk, with a deep admiration and devotion to the teachings of the Buddha, and particularly to his teachings on compassion and the understanding of the deeper nature of reality. I do not have any pride in my own ability to fully represent the rich spiritual teachings of the Buddha, however I do try my best to shoulder the responsibility history has placed on me by sharing my personal understanding of the Buddhist teachings with as many people as possible.

Many reading these teachings will, as their principal aim, be seeking methods to transform their mind. On the part of the teacher it is desirable, if possible, for him or her to have complete knowledge of the topics on which he or she is teaching. On my part, as far as I am concerned, I cannot claim to have full, complete knowledge of the topics I am dealing with here. However, the text we are studying is predominately about the doctrine of emptiness, and I do have a deep admiration for the philosophy of emptiness, and whenever I have the opportunity, I try to reflect on it as much as I can. Based on my little experience—I can claim at least a little experience—I have a sense that it is a living philosophy and that an understanding of emptiness does have an effect. Also, I feel emotionally connected to the idea of emptiness. This is as much of a qualification as I can claim for teaching this text.

Intellect and Faith

For all readers, whether you have developed a deep interest in Buddhism and are embarking on a spiritual path to explore the rich teachings of the Buddha, or whether you are just beginning, it is important not to be blinded by faith alone—taking everything on board simply on the basis of faith. If you do, there is the danger of losing your critical faculty. Rather, the object of your faith or devotion must be discovered through a personal understanding derived through critical reflection. If, as a result of your critical reflection, you develop a sense of deep conviction—then your faith can develop. Confidence and faith developed on the basis of reason will certainly be very firm and reliable. Without using your intellect, your faith in the Buddha's teachings will simply be an unreasoned faith with no grounding in your own understanding.

It is important to study to expand your own personal understanding of the Buddha's teachings. Nagarjuna, the second-century Indian master, states that both faith and intelligence are crucial factors for our spiritual development, and of the two, faith is the foundation. He clearly states, however, that for faith to have sufficient power to drive our spiritual progress, we need intelligence, a faculty that can enable us to recognize the right path and to cultivate deep insights. Your understanding should not remain, however, merely at the level of knowledge and intellect. Rather, it should be integrated into your heart and mind so that there is a direct impact on your conduct. Otherwise your study of Buddhism will be purely intellectual and will have no effect on your attitudes, your conduct, or your way of life.

The Root Text

In Tibetan Buddhism the root texts, such as the sutras and tantras, are the original words of the Buddha himself. In addition, there is the Tengyur, the extensive collection of treatises composed by authoritative Indian scholars. There are also thousands of commentarial works written by many great masters from all four traditions of Tibetan Buddhism. The root text we are using for this present teaching is "Wisdom," the ninth chapter of *The Way of the Bodhisattva (Bodhicharyavatara),* written in the eighth century by the great Indian master Shantideva.

I received the transmission of this text from the late Khunu Rinpoche, Tenzin Gyaltsen, who was a great meditator and spiritual teacher. He specialized in the practice of generating the altruistic mind of awakening, based on Shantideva's text. Khunu Rinpoche received the transmission from the renowned Dza Paltrül Rinpoche.

I will be using two important references as the basis of my commentary on Shantideva's text. The first is by Khenpo Künpal and reflects the terminology of Nyingma, the Old Translation school. The other is by Minyak Künsö, who although a student of Paltrül Rinpoche, was himself a follower of the Geluk school and therefore used the terminology of the Geluk tradition. As I give the exposition of the root text itself, I will also highlight where these two experts give divergent interpretations of Shantideva's ninth chapter. Let's see how it goes!

2. THE BUDDHIST CONTEXT

Historical Background

The compassionate and skillful teacher Buddha Shakyamuni lived in India more than 2,500 years ago. He taught various techniques and methods of spiritual transformation, and did so according to the diverse dispositions, interests, and mentalities of the sentient beings he taught.

A rich spiritual and philosophical tradition developed that was enhanced and maintained by continuous lineages of great Indian masters such as Nagarjuna and Asanga. It came to full flowering in India and later went to many other countries in Asia. In Tibet, Buddhism began to flourish in the seventh and eighth centuries. A great many personalities were part of this historical process, including the Indian abbot Shantarakshita, the teacher Padmasambhava, and the then Tibetan monarch Trisong Detsen. From this period onward the development of Buddhism in Tibet was extremely rapid. As in India, successive lineages of great Tibetan masters contributed tremendously to spreading the Buddha's teachings across the breadth of the entire country. Over time, and due to Tibetan geographical factors, four major Buddhist schools evolved in Tibet. This led to a divergence in the choice of terminology and to the emphasis placed on the various aspects of Buddhist meditative practices and views.

The first of the four schools is the Nyingma, the "old translation" school, which began from the time of Padmasambhava. Since the period of the great translator Rinchen Sangpo, the other three schools, known collectively as the "new translation" schools, evolved, giving rise to the Kagyü, Sakya, and Geluk. What is common to these four traditions is that they are all complete forms of Buddhism. Not only does each contain the essence of the teachings of the Hinayana, each lineage also contains the essence of Mahayana and Vajrayana Buddhism.

The Buddhist Path

For those who are not Buddhist or who are new to the teachings, it may be of benefit for me to provide a general overview of the Buddhist path.

All of us, as human beings with feelings and consciousness, instinctively seek happiness and wish to overcome suffering. Along with that innate aspiration, we also have a right to fulfill this fundamental aim. Regardless of whether we succeed or fail, all our pursuits in life are, in one way or another, directed toward the fulfillment of this basic desire. This is the case for all of us who seek spiritual liberation—whether nirvana or salvation, whether we believe in rebirth or not. What is obvious is that our experiences of pain and pleasure, happiness and unhappiness, are all intimately related to our own attitudes, thoughts, and emotions. In fact we could say that all of them arise from the mind. We see, therefore, in the teachings of all the major religious traditions of the world, an emphasis on spiritual paths based on a transformation of the heart and mind.

What is unique to the Buddhist teaching is that underlying its entire spiritual path is the premise that there is a profound disparity between our perceptions of reality and the way things really are. This disparity at the heart of our being leads to all sorts of psychological confusion, emotional afflictions, disappointments, and frustrations—in a word, suffering. Even in our day-to-day life, we are constantly exposed to situations where we feel deceived, disillusioned, and so on. One of the most effective antidotes to this type of situation is to consciously develop our knowledge, widen our perspectives, and become more familiar with the world. By doing this, we will find ourselves more able to cope with adversities and to be not so constantly in a state of frustration and disillusionment.

Similarly, at the spiritual level too, it is crucial to broaden our perspectives and develop a genuine insight into the true nature of reality. In this way, the fundamental misperception, or ignorance, that permeates our perceptions of the world and our existence can be eliminated. Because of this, in Buddhism, we find discussions on the nature of two truths that form the basic structure of reality. Based on this understanding of reality, the various levels of spiritual paths and grounds are explained. They can all be realized within ourselves on the basis of genuine insight. So, in Buddhism, when we embark upon a spiritual path toward enlightenment, we need to do so by cultivating genuine insight into the deeper nature of reality. Without such a grounding, there is no possibility of attaining heightened spiritual realizations, and our spiritual endeavor may become a mere fantasy built on no foundation at all.

Causality and the Four Noble Truths

When the Buddha gave his first public sermon following his full awakening, he did so within the framework of the four noble truths. These are the truths of suffering, the origin of suffering, the ceasing of suffering, and the path that leads to the cessation of suffering.

At the heart of the teaching on the four noble truths is the principle of causality. With this knowledge, the four truths can be divided into two pairs of a cause and an effect. The first pair is about what we do not desire, and concerns our experience of suffering. The second pair of cause and effect is about our happiness and serenity. In other words, the first truth of suffering is the effect of the second truth, its origin; and similarly, the third truth of cessation, which is the state of liberation, or freedom from suffering, is the effect of the fourth truth, the path leading to that state of freedom. The end to suffering is the goal of the spiritual aspirant, and is true freedom, or happiness. These teachings reflect a deep understanding of the nature of reality.

Three Kinds of Suffering

The truth of suffering refers to more than just our experience of our very obvious sufferings, such as the sensation of pain; animals also recognize this as undesirable. There is a second level of suffering, known as the *suffering of change,* which refers to what we more often regard as pleasurable sensations. Based on our own day-to-day experience of the transient nature of these pleasurable sensations, we can also recognize this level of suffering, for we can see in its very nature that dissatisfaction must always be a part of it.

The third level of suffering is known as the *pervasive suffering of conditioning*. This is much more difficult for us to recognize as suffering. To do so requires a degree of deep reflection. We have all sorts of preconceptions, thoughts, prejudices, fears, and hopes. Such thought processes and emotions give rise to certain states of mind, which in turn propel various actions, many of which are destructive and often cause further mental confusion and emotional distress. All of these afflictive thoughts and emotions are thus related to certain actions—mental, verbal, or physical. Some actions, however, are not specifically motivated by any negative or positive states of mind; rather they come from a state of indifference, a neutral state of mind. Such actions are normally not powerful and leave little impact. In contrast, actions that are driven by strong motivation or emotion—be it positive or negative—leave a definite impression on both our state of mind and our behavior. Especially if the motivation is negative, the imprint on both mind and body tends to be very marked. So, based on our own daily experience, we can infer a causal connection between our thoughts and emotions and their expression in our outward behavior. This cycle of thoughts and emotions producing negative behaviors, which in turn condition further afflicted thoughts and emotions, is a process that perpetuates itself without any special effort from our side. The third level of suffering refers to the nature of our existence as fundamentally enmeshed in an unsatisfactory cycle. When Buddhism speaks of the possibility of an end to suffering, it means freedom from this third level of suffering.

The Potential for Freedom

The questions could be raised here: "Is it ever possible to change the very nature of our existence, formed as it is by contaminated physical and mental components? Is it at all possible to exist without being enmeshed in such a conditioned existence?" In discussing cessation, Buddhism is pointing to the possibility of freedom, meaning the total elimination of all negative aspects of our psyche, the possibility of complete freedom from all suffering. This is an issue that requires serious thought on the part of a practitioner.

In the first turning of the wheel of Dharma, the Buddha talked about cessation, however it is only in the Mahayana teachings of the second and the third turnings of the wheel of Dharma that the nature of cessation and liberation are explained to their full extent. In the second turning of the wheel of Dharma, principally in the perfection of wisdom *(prajnaparamita)* scriptures, the Buddha explained that the essential nature of the mind is pure. From this viewpoint, our various troublesome emotions and thoughts are adventitious, that is they are not an integral part of the essential nature of the mind and can therefore be removed.

As practicing Buddhists we should critically reflect on the following questions: "Do our afflictive states of mind—and in particular our underlying misperception and ignorance, which has us grasping at the intrinsic existence of phenomena—accord with the nature of reality? Or are our afflictions distorted states of mind that have no grounding in valid experience or reality?" Through this reflection it will become evident that it is first necessary to examine in general whether phenomena possess—as they most often appear to—an intrinsic and independent reality. Do individual people, things, and events each exist separately, in their own right? In the perfection of wisdom scriptures we find an extensive discussion concerning the absence of the intrinsic existence of all phenomena. These scriptures state that although we may perceive and experience both our own existence and other phenomena as having intrinsic existence, if we probe with deeper analysis, we find that our perception of their concrete and independent existence is distorted and therefore false. We will find that this perception is in fact a misperception and has no grounding in reality.

It follows that all the ensuing states affected by this type of misperception, such as the afflictive emotions—anger, hatred, desire, jealousy, and so on—are also devoid of a valid correlation with reality. Because this underlying root cause, the fundamental ignorance, which mistakenly perceives all things and events as being intrinsically real, is distorted, it can therefore be corrected, through insight. This implies the possibility of putting an end to the whole cycle of unenlightened existence caused by ignorance. The effects of ignorance, those contaminated aggregates of body and mind, which bind us in this unenlightened existence, can be eliminated as well. The state of being utterly free from the entanglement resulting from this fundamental misperception is nirvana, or true liberation. In this way the Buddha presented the teachings on the four noble truths. The Buddha explored and further developed the themes of the four noble truths in his teachings on the twelve links of dependent origination.

Dependent Origination

In the *Dependent Origination Sutra* Buddha states:

> If there is this, that ensues;
> Because this came into being, that came into being.
> It is thus: Due to ignorance volition arises...[7]

In other words, in order for a particular event or experience to take place, there must be a cause, and the cause itself must be existent. That cause will also be an effect of a preceding cause, because if it is not itself a product, then it will lack the potential or capacity to produce any results. So the cause itself has to be a product of another cause. Therefore, the Buddha said that because this cause arises, the effect is produced. And not only must the cause have a cause, the cause must also correlate to the effect. It is not true that just anything can produce everything; rather, only certain causes can lead to certain types of effects.

Following on from this, Buddha stated that the presence of fundamental ignorance leads to *karma,* or action. Our undesirable experiences of suffering, such as pain, fear, and death, are all basically effects produced by corresponding causes. So in order to put an end to these sufferings, we have to put an end to the relevant sequence of causes and effects. Buddha explained how, within the framework of the twelve links of dependent origination, the earlier elements in the causal sequence give rise to the later elements. He also explained the process of reversing the twelve links of dependent origination. In other words, by putting an end to the earlier elements, we can eliminate the later elements. So, by completely cutting the causal root—eliminating our fundamental ignorance—we will finally come to experience total freedom from all suffering and its origin.

In the twelve links of dependent origination, ignorance is listed as the first cause. This, I feel, reflects the basic truth that we all instinctively desire happiness and seek to avoid suffering. No one needs to teach us this innate desire. However, although we possess this natural aspiration to seek happiness and overcome suffering, we nonetheless find ourselves without lasting happiness and enmeshed in suffering. This indicates that there is something wrong in our way of being. We are ignorant of the means to fulfill our basic aspiration for happiness. So the insight that we gain from the teachings of the twelve links of dependent origination—that ignorance is the root cause of our suffering—is indeed true.

There are of course differing interpretations among Buddhist thinkers, such as Asanga and Dharmakirti, about the nature of this fundamental ignorance. Predominately this ignorance is thought of not simply as a state of not knowing, but rather as a state of active misunderstanding, meaning we think we have understood when we haven't. It is a distorted way of understanding reality where we experience the things and events of the world as if each one had some kind of independent, intrinsic existence.

Insight

The term *ignorance,* used generally, may refer to both negative and neutral states of mind. By *fundamental ignorance,* however, we mean that which is the root cause of our cyclic existence. We are referring to a state of mind that is distorted. Because it is distorted, misapprehending the nature of reality, it follows that the way to eliminate this ignorance is to generate insight into the true nature of reality, to see through the deception created by the ignorance. Such an insight can be gained only by experiencing the utter groundlessness of the viewpoint created by this distorted state of mind. Merely praying, "May I be rid of this fundamental ignorance" will not bring the desired goal. We need to cultivate insight.

It is only through generating such an insight and penetrating into the nature of reality that we will be able to dispel this fundamental misperception. By this insight, or wisdom, I am referring to what is known in Buddhist terminology as the understanding of *emptiness* or *no-self.* There are diverse interpretations of what is meant by the terms *emptiness, no-self, selflessness,* and *identitylessness* in the Buddhist teachings. However, here I am using these terms to refer to the emptiness of intrinsic existence. Grasping at the opposite—that things and events possess some kind of intrinsic or independent existence—is the fundamental ignorance. The profound insight that arises with the realization of the absence of any such intrinsic existence is known as the *true path.*

In the second turning of the wheel of Dharma, mainly in the perfection of wisdom sutras, the Buddha states that our ignorance lies at the root of all our afflictions and confusion—our negative thoughts and emotions and the suffering they cause. He states that our fundamental ignorance and the afflictions it causes are not the essential nature of the mind. These afflictions are fundamentally separate from the essential character of mind, which is defined as "luminous and knowing." The essential nature of mind is pure, and the capacity to perceive things and events is a natural function of the mind. This description of the mind's natural purity and its capacity for cognition are emphasized in the perfection of wisdom sutras, which present the essential nature of mind as having the character of *clear light*.

PRACTICING WISDOM

The Basis of Success

For a practicing Buddhist the final spiritual objective is *nirvana,* the state of the mind that has been cleansed of all its distressed and deluded states. This is possible through a gradual process of practicing, and it requires time. If we are to possess the vital faculties necessary to pursue our spiritual journey, then right from the initial stages of this path to nirvana, or liberation, we have to ensure that our form of existence and our lifestyle are fully conducive to Dharma practice.

In his *Four Hundred Verses on the Middle Way (Chatuhshatakashastra),* Aryadeva presents a specific procedure for proceeding on the path to enlightenment.[8] This suggests that it is important to psursue the path in a systematic order, beginning by refraining from negative actions and maintaining an ethically sound way of life. This is to ensure the attainment of a favorable rebirth so that we will be able to continue to pursue our spiritual path in the future. Aryadeva states that the first phase of the path is to avert the effects of negative and troublesome states of mind as they manifest in our behavior, because this safeguards us against taking unfavorable rebirth in the next life. In the next phase, the emphasis is placed on generating insight into the nature of no-self or emptiness. The final phase of the path is the total elimination of all distorted views and the overcoming of even the most subtle obstructions to knowledge.

It is on the basis of understanding the four noble truths that we will be able to develop a real understanding of the nature of the Three Jewels of Buddha, Dharma, and Sangha. Through deeply understanding the four noble truths, we will be able to genuinely recognize the possibility of attaining nirvana, or true liberation. When we understand that our afflicted and negative states of mind can be removed, we will then be able to recognize the real possibility of attaining true liberation—not just in general, but in relation to one's own self. We will sense, as individuals, that this freedom is actually within reach through our own realization. Once we gain such conviction, we will understand that we can also overcome the habitual patterns formed by our deluded states of mind. In this way we generate a conviction in the possibility of attaining full enlightenment. And once we develop such a conviction, we will then be able to appreciate the true value of taking refuge in the Buddha, Dharma, and Sangha.

Our first expression of going for refuge in the Three Jewels—our first commitment—is to lead our life in accordance with karma, the law of cause and effect. This entails living an ethically disciplined life where we restrain from the ten negative actions—the three physical misdeeds of killing, stealing, and engaging in sexual misconduct, the four verbal misdeeds of lying, divisive speech, harsh speech, and gossip, and the three mental misdeeds of covetousness, ill will, and harboring wrong views. The second step is to overcome grasping at self, or intrinsic existence. This stage primarily involves the practice of the three higher trainings—ethical discipline, meditation, and wisdom. In the third and final phase, we need to overcome not only our afflictive and negative states of mind, but we must overcome even the predispositions and habits formed by these deluded states.

This final stage is achieved through combining insight into emptiness—the ultimate nature of reality—with universal compassion. In order for that to be achieved, our realization of emptiness must be complemented with the skillful methods of attainment, including such factors as the altruistic aspiration to attain buddhahood for the sake of all sentient beings, universal compassion, and loving-kindness. It is only through complementing our wisdom realizing emptiness with these factors of skillful means that we will actually be able to develop wisdom powerful enough to eliminate all the predispositions and habits formed by our deluded mental and emotional states. This will then lead to the realization of the final state, buddhahood.

When our realization of emptiness arises on the basis of the complete preliminaries, it becomes an antidote powerful enough to eliminate all the obscurations to full enlightenment. Right at the beginning of the ninth chapter, Shantideva states that all the other aspects of Dharma practice have been taught by the Buddha for the sake of generating wisdom. Therefore, if your objective is to bring about an end to suffering, then you must develop the wisdom of emptiness.

MEDITATION

Meditate here on the understanding of the four noble truths as we have discussed them so far. In particular, reflect how fundamental ignorance keeps us locked in a cycle of suffering and how insight into the true nature of reality allows us to eradicate the negative thoughts and emotions from our mind. Reflect how insight into emptiness combined with the skillful means of compassion and the altruistic intention can even eliminate the subtle predispositions toward negative actions.

3. THE TWO TRUTHS

COMMENTARY

First, I would like to point out the broad sections of Shantideva's root text that I will be using as the basis for my exposition of the ninth chapter, "Wisdom." According to the commentaries by Khenpo Künpal and Minyak Künsö, the ninth chapter is divided into the following three segments:

1. The necessity of cultivating the wisdom of emptiness (verse 1)
2. A detailed explanation of how to cultivate this wisdom (verses 2–150)
3. A concise explanation of how to realize emptiness (verses 151–67)

The Necessity of Wisdom

And now we can begin with verse 1, where Shantideva states unequivocally the necessity of practicing wisdom:

> 1. All these branches of the Doctrine
> The Powerful Lord expounded for the sake of wisdom.
> Therefore they must generate this wisdom
> Who wish to have an end of suffering.

In brief, all aspects of the teachings of the Buddha are intended to lead individuals to the state of full enlightenment. All the teachings finally converge on this point. Because of this, either directly or indirectly, all the teachings are related to the path of generating wisdom. This is why Shantideva here says that all the branches of the teachings are for gaining wisdom.

According to the Middle Way philosophy of the Mahayana tradition, the realization of emptiness is indispensable even to attain liberation from cyclic existence. This point is stated repeatedly in Shantideva's text. When we speak of attaining freedom from suffering, it is crucial that our understanding of suffering is not limited to the suffering of painful sensations. Our understanding must also include the origins of suffering, such as the afflictive emotions and thoughts.

The second segment (verses 2–150) is a detailed explanation of how to develop the realization of emptiness, and it has three sections. The first of these sections (verses 2–39) is divided into three subsections, each one concerned with specific aspects of the two truths. They are:

1. definitions of the two truths (verse 2)
2. the different kinds of individuals who establish the two truths (verses 3–4ab)
3. dealing with objections on how the two truths are posited (verses 4cd–39)

Definitions

First is the definitions of the two truths, which Shantideva presents in the second verse.

> 2. Relative and absolute,
> These the two truths are declared to be.
> The absolute is not within the reach of intellect,
> For intellect is grounded in the relative.

As I mentioned above, since there is this basic discrepancy between the way we perceive things and the way things really exist, there is an illusion-like quality to our perception of our own existence and of the world around us. In order to develop true insight into the ultimate nature of reality, it becomes important to understand the *two truths,* which refers to the twofold nature of reality. We find the term *two truths* used also in non-Buddhist literature, such as the philosophical writings of many ancient Indian schools that also upheld notions of spiritual freedom. However, the doctrine of the two truths referred to by Shantideva is that described in the writings of the Indian Middle Way, or Madhyamaka, school, and in particular its subschool known as the Prasangika-Madhyamaka.

Past Buddhist thinkers diverge in explaining the reason for the division into two truths. Some maintain that the basis of division is our conventional experience of the world. Others, such as Butön Rinpoche, take truth in its entirety as the basis of the division. They therefore see the two truths as two aspects of truth in general. A third group of scholars take knowable objects as the basis, which they then divide into two aspects, conventional truth and ultimate truth. This third approach is based on more authoritative Indian sources, such as Shantideva's *Compendium of Deeds (Shikshasamuchaya),* in which the author explicitly cites knowable objects as the basis of the division between the two truths.

In Minyak Künsö's commentary, the author states that the two truths are presented from the point of view of two different perspectives. From the perspective of our everyday experience, the reality of the world is conventional and relative. From the perspective of the way things ultimately exist, the reality of the world is emptiness, which is the ultimate, or absolute, truth. The two truths are understood then as two different perspectives on one and the same world.

In his *Supplement to the Middle Way (Madhyamakavatara),* Chandrakirti states that all things and events have two natures, or aspects. The conventional, or relative, aspect is known from our phenomenal experience, and the ultimate nature of things is perceived from the point of view of the ultimate perspective. So here too we find that the two truths are defined in terms of two different perspectives. One is from the perspective of our everyday experience, and the other is from the perspective of the true insight into the ultimate nature of reality.

In this view, when we examine the nature of the reality of things and events—everyday objects such as tables, chairs, vases, and flowers—the degree of reality that we perceive at the level of our phenomenal experience relates to their relative truth. And so long as we remain content within this framework, we remain at the level of phenomenal experience and conventional validity. The moment that we are not content with the validity of the conventional framework and seek to go beyond its confines, we are then searching for a deeper or truer essence or core identity. Yet what we find through the ensuing analysis is that things and events are actually unfindable. When engaged in this way, we are relating to the world, to things and events, at their ultimate level, their total emptiness. This is their emptiness of intrinsic existence, the absence of any identity and existence of things and events in their own right. At this point we find that the two truths are most clearly understood as two different perspectives on the things and events that make up the world.

The commentary by Künpal reflects the viewpoint of the Nyingma school. One of the characteristics of its style of presentation can be seen clearly in Mipham's (1846–1912) commentary on Shantarakshita's *Ornament of the Middle Way (Madhyamakalamkara),* where he distinguishes between the Prasangika-Madhyamaka and Svatantrika-Madhyamaka schools on the basis of their understanding of the two truths. He states, however, that the two Middle Way schools equally maintain ultimate truth as being beyond the scope of intellect, and as such it is not considered to be an object of the intellect. According to Mipham, anything that is an object of the intellect must necessarily be relative and conventional.

Reality and Intellectual Understanding

Among Tibetan commentators there are two different interpretations of the line, "The absolute is not within the reach of intellect." One is to adopt an understanding of the absolute or ultimate truth from two different perspectives and to maintain that the actual ultimate truth lies beyond the scope of the intellect, the cognition of an ordinary being. That is Khenpo Künpal's interpretation. Another understanding of this crucial line comes from the writings of Tsongkhapa.[9] In his view the ultimate truth is not an object of an intellect that is dualistic, whose object of cognition is the relative and conventional. Instead, the ultimate truth is an object of a direct perception or experience that is totally free of dualistic elaborations and concepts. Therefore, according to Tsongkhapa also, the two truths are defined on the basis of two different perspectives.

According to Tsongkhapa's understanding, we can read the second verse of the ninth chapter as presenting the definitions of the two truths. The reference to ultimate reality as not being within the reach of the intellect provides the definition of ultimate truth. So we now read Shantideva as defining ultimate truth as that aspect of reality that is an object of a direct perception that is totally free of dualistic and conceptual elaborations. In contrast, the level of reality that lies within the scope of dualistic cognition is relative and conventional. In this way, we see Shantideva's passage as defining the two truths.

When Mipham, in his exposition on Shantarakshita's *The Ornament of the Middle Way,* comments on the line, "The absolute is not within the reach of the intellect," he states that although the mere negation of the intrinsic existence of phenomena is an object of the intellect, the emptiness that is the union of appearance and reality remains inaccessible to the intellect. It is important to note that when we speak of emptiness here, in the context of *Bodhicharyavatara,* we are doing so as it is understood within the sutra system. However, when we speak of emptiness in the context of tantra, intellect or cognition has a different meaning. Tantra speaks of various levels and subtleties in the wisdom realizing emptiness, and by extension of different levels of freedom from dualistic elaborations.

It is also important to recognize that the scope of the two truths includes all things and events—the entire spectrum of reality is exhausted. In other words, there is no third possibility. There is nothing in the expanse of reality that is neither of the two truths.

A Sequence for Understanding the Two Truths

As for the sequence in which the two truths are established, let us take the example of an everyday object such as a flower. First, the object, the flower, will appear to the mind, and then, on the basis of that appearance, we are able to examine its real nature. Shantideva's *Compendium of Deeds* is replete with quotations from the sutras where the Buddha talks in great detail about the causal principle that exists in nature—how certain causes and conditions lead to certain effects and situations. First in these scriptures are extensive treatments of the conventional level of reality. By examining how certain causes and conditions give rise to certain events, we can become more familiar with this world of multiplicity, which in turn has a direct effect on our experience. It is only on the basis of such solid grounding in understanding how things work in the phenomenal world of conventional reality that the analysis of the ultimate nature of reality can be brought into the picture. Once we have developed confidence in our understanding of the world of conventional truth, then we can enter productively into the examination of the ultimate truth. We will then be able to fully recognize the discrepancy that exists between our perception of the world and the way things really are.

To fully appreciate the extent of the discrepancy between our perceptions and reality, it is essential that we successfully challenge the idea of concrete reality that we ordinarily project onto things and events. This is our belief and experience that things and events exist in their own right and that they possess some kind of intrinsic identity and existence. It is through this process of negating this belief that we arrive at a deeper understanding of the ultimate truth, of emptiness.

Sameness and Difference

There is then the question of whether the two truths are different or identical. On this issue there are also various viewpoints. For example, Butön maintains that the two truths are different in terms of their natures, whereas Tsongkhapa, citing Nagarjuna's *Commentary on the Awakening Mind (Bodhichittavivarana)* as his authority, states that the two truths, though having conventionally distinct identities, are of the same nature. Like the distinction in Buddhist philosophy between the properties of being impermanent and of being a product, the distinction between the two truths pertains to two distinct perspectives on the same entity. Both truths relate to one and the same world. It is on the basis of adopting the two different perspectives that we are able to distinguish the natures and identities of the two truths.

The identity of the two truths and their sharing the same nature is also referred to in the *Heart Sutra*. The well-known passage reads: "Form is emptiness, emptiness is form; there is no emptiness apart from form, and there is no form apart from emptiness." The sutra goes on to state that all things and events possess this characteristic of emptiness.[10] When we speak of the emptiness of form and other phenomena, we should not have the idea that emptiness is some kind of external quality that is projected upon objects. Rather we need to understand their emptiness as a function of their dependently arisen nature.

When we analyze carefully, we find that both the physical existence and the identity of a form, for example, arise in dependence on other factors, such as that form's causes and conditions. Beyond the interrelated factors that constitute its existence, we cannot speak of an autonomous, independent identity or existence of any given phenomenon. This is not to say that the form does not exist at all, for clearly we can experience it, perceive it, and interact with it. At the level of multiplicity, our day-to-day experience, there *is* a form. But this form does not exist intrinsically—with its own discrete, independent reality. It exists only through relation with other factors, such as its causes, conditions, and various constituent parts. This indicates that form is utterly devoid of an independent status. Given that it is devoid of independent nature, it follows that it is dependent upon other factors. It is susceptible to transformation, and therefore, through interacting with other factors, it assumes different characteristics. The form's absence of any independent nature—this characteristic of being empty of intrinsic existence—is its ultimate truth. And this is why the Buddha states in the *Heart Sutra* that "form is emptiness, emptiness is form."

Two Kinds of Selflessness

When speaking of the ultimate truth, there are two major divisions: the selflessness, or identitylessness, of persons and the selflessness or identitylessness of phenomena. Chandrakirti states in the *Supplement to the Middle Way* that the division into selflessness of persons and selflessness of phenomena is made not on the basis of two totally different kinds of selflessness. Rather it is done on the basis that in the world there are two principal categories of phenomena—subjects and objects. So "phenomena" refers here to the world, to things and events, and "person" to sentient beings. Based on this division of reality, we find the scriptures present two corresponding types of ultimate truth.

This is the position of the Prasangika-Madhyamaka. Other schools of thought, such as the Svatantrika-Madhyamaka and other Buddhist philosophical schools, maintain that there is a substantive difference between the selflessness of persons and the selflessness of phenomena. In the Prasangika-Madhyamaka, although there is an acceptance of various degrees of subtlety in understanding the selflessness of persons, in the final analysis, both the selflessness of persons and the selflessness of phenomena are equally subtle. We also find ultimate truth divided into lists of four, sixteen, and twenty emptinesses. These different taxonomies provide various ways of talking about emptiness. For example, emptiness may be divided into internal emptiness, external emptiness, emptiness of both, and so on, often ending with the emptiness of emptiness. The point of identifying the emptiness of emptiness as a distinct category is that, since emptiness is presented as the ultimate truth, there is a danger of grasping onto emptiness as an absolute. The Buddha states therefore that even emptiness itself is empty of intrinsic existence.

True and False Conventions

Conventional, or relative, truth is divided into true and false conventions. According to the Prasangika-Madhyamikas,[11] however, since self-existence, or intrinsic existence, is denied even on the conventional level, the division of conventional truth into true and false can only be made from a certain perspective. In reality, there is no actual division within the conventional world. But using such a perspective, we can speak about unreal and real perception, and we can characterize certain types of phenomenal experience as true and others as false.

Etymologies

Let us now look at the etymology of the two truths. The term *conventional truth* implies a level of truth affirmed by the conventional subject or knower that rests on the mistaken belief in the true existence of things. Because of this, the Prasangika-Madhyamika does not accept the *truth* in the context of conventional truth as referring to truth in the real sense. So *truth* here does not refer to some correspondence with the way things really are. Rather it refers to truth within a certain limited, relative framework. "Truth" in this conventional framework refers to a truth constructed by a particular viewpoint, and that viewpoint is our perception—or rather, our misperception—of the world, wherein we perceive all phenomena as if they possessed some kind of intrinsic reality. This deluded perception perceives people, things, and events as inherently and truly existing. From this point of view, the things in our conventional experience are seen to be valid, reliable, truthful, and enjoying some kind of discrete, independent, and objective existence. The conventional truth is also referred to as the *veiled truth* or *concealed truth*.

This etymological explanation might appear to be providing some degree of validity to the perspective of our deluded states of mind. However, it is simply an etymological explanation. In actual fact, things that appear to be true from this deluded perspective need not even constitute a relative truth. For example, even emptiness is grasped at as being valid from this deluded perspective, but that does not mean that emptiness can be accepted as a conventional or relative truth. Therefore, the delusory point of view from which phenomena are seen as real cannot be accepted as valid. We need therefore to find a perspective that has the ability to establish the validity of the conventional world. The perspective from which the reality of conventional truth is established cannot be that of a misperceiving or distorted state of mind.

Let us now turn to the meaning of truth in the context of *ultimate truth*. In his *Clear Words (Prasannapada),* Chandrakirti states that the term *ultimate* refers to both the object, emptiness, and to the direct experience of it. So, from this viewpoint, the "ultimate" in the context of ultimate truth refers both to the subjective experience and to the object, emptiness, as well. To go further, emptiness is both the ultimate and the truth being referred to when we speak of the ultimate truth. For example, Chandrakirti says that emptiness is the "meaning" or the "truth" *(don),* and it is also the "ultimate" *(dampa).* So here we see a convergence of the terms *ultimate* and *truth*.

Without understanding the nature of these two truths—the conventional and the ultimate—it is difficult to fully appreciate the distinction between appearance and reality, that is, the discrepancy we experience between our perception and the way things really are. Without a deep understanding of this fact, we won't be in a position to get at the root of our fundamental ignorance.

Emptiness and Compassion

Of course, there are various specific antidotes to the afflictions—such as meditation on love to counter hatred, meditation on the impurity of our body to counter desire, and so on. These various techniques can reduce different types of afflictive emotions and thoughts. However, as Dharmakirti states in his *Valid Cognition,* these methods only deal with the obvious manifestations of these afflictions. That is, they only indirectly influence our afflictions and the fundamental ignorance underlying them. They have no capacity to act as a direct counterforce to our fundamental misperception. It is only by generating true insight into the ultimate nature of reality that we will be able to get at the root of our confusion—our deluded way of perceiving—and the suffering it gives rise to. Without developing a full understanding of the two truths, we will not be able to gain deep insight into the true nature of reality. By developing a deep understanding of the two truths, we will be able to recognize the various distinctions that exist among our perceptions of the world, and also in our cognitive and emotional states. On the basis of this insight we can enhance the capacity and force of our positive mental states, such as compassion, love, tolerance, and so on, and at the same time reduce the force of our negative and afflictive states, such as anger, hatred, jealousy, and strong attachment. Since all these delusory and afflictive states are rooted in our belief in an intrinsic existence of the world, by generating true insight into emptiness we will be able to cut the root of all these delusory states. We will be in a position to fully develop and enhance the positive potentials that exist in our mind and reduce and eventually eliminate our negative and afflictive emotions and thoughts. This is one of the primary benefits of developing a profound understanding of the two truths.

Citing Nagarjuna's text, Khenpo Künpal states in his commentary that the realization of emptiness and the arising of great compassion within one's heart are simultaneous.[12] He comments that as our understanding of emptiness deepens, so too our compassion toward other sentient beings will increase. It is difficult however to see the automatic connection between the realization of emptiness and the arising of nondiscriminatory compassion toward all sentient beings. However, it does appear to be true that the deeper our realization of emptiness, the deeper our recognition of the possibility of ending our suffering. And as we deepen our conviction that every sentient being has the potential to be free from suffering, then of course our compassion toward other sentient beings will increase. For then we know there is a way out, and our compassion for sentient beings—who are bound in this cyclic existence due to their ignorance of the way to be free from it—will naturally increase. So, as our realization of emptiness deepens, I feel that there is a corresponding and definite increase in the strength of our compassion toward others.

Therefore, if as an individual meditator you have a sense that your realization of emptiness is deepening yet there is no corresponding increase in your compassion toward others, then this is perhaps an indication that your understanding of emptiness is not really profound or genuine. As I often say, meditation on emptiness alone is not something to be admired. It is also crucial, in our day-to-day interaction with others, to be able to relate in an ethical and a compassionate way. So if your understanding of emptiness does not contribute positively in any way toward this goal, there is no worth in it at all. What is there to be so admired about a realization of emptiness that does not lead to greater compassion?

We should not have the notion that buddhahood is a state of total apathy, devoid of feeling, emotion, and empathy toward other sentient beings. For if that were the case, there would be nothing admirable about the state of buddhahood. Meditation on emptiness is not some kind of escapism, refusing to deal with the diversity and complexity of the conventional and relative world. The aim is to be able to relate with the phenomenal world in a correct and meaningful way.

This then concludes a brief exposition of the nature and role of the two truths.

Two Kinds of People

The root text next discusses the viewpoints of various kinds of individuals in regard to their understanding of the tenets and practice of Buddhism, such as the two truths. The text reads:

> 3. Two kinds of people are to be distinguished:
> Meditative thinkers and ordinary folk;
> The common views of ordinary people
> Are superseded by the views of meditators.
>
> 4ab. And within the ranks of meditators,
> The lower, in degrees of insight, are confuted by the higher.

Having made the case that the understanding of the two truths is crucial, Shantideva's root text goes on to explain that there are two principal types of people who will be dealing with the two truths, the meditator and the ordinary person. In Tibetan, the word for *ordinary folk* is *jiktenpa,* while the Tibetan term for meditator, in this context, is *naljorpa* and refers to people who possess a heightened perspective. *Jik* suggests something that is transient, something that is susceptible to cessation, and *ten* refers to a basis or foundation. So the term *jikten* implies a lack of permanence, and *jiktenpa* refers to a person or a transient being. The idea of *jik,* disintegration, negates the possibility of permanence, or eternity. By reflecting on this expression we can understand that there is no absolute, eternal, unitary self.

Ordinary folk here also includes those who follow philosophical tenets that uphold some form of realist perspective on the question of the ultimate nature of reality. This includes the followers of all the non-Buddhist ancient Indian schools and the followers of some tenet systems among the Buddhist schools. The Vaibhashikas, for instance, believe in an atomistic world—an objective, independent world constituted by indivisible atoms. So in their tenets there is a belief in the substantial reality of things and events. The views of this school are negated by the

Sautrantika school. They maintain that there are certain aspects of reality—such as mental constructs like the abstract composites—whose reality can be posited only from the perspective of thought and conceptualization. So they argue that we cannot give absolute objective status to things and events. The tenets of this school are again disputed by other Buddhist schools, and so on. This is what Shantideva means when he asserts that the perspectives of one are confuted or invalidated by the perspective of another. Even among the contemplatives, due to the different levels of their spiritual experience, the perspectives of those contemplatives at higher levels will supersede the perspectives of those at lower levels of realization.

Let us now look more closely at Shantideva's statement that the perspectives of ordinary people are invalidated and superseded by the perspective of the meditators. I believe that the manner in which one perspective supersedes and invalidates the other must be understood in terms of the level of the development of reasoning. Naturally, in a discourse among the Buddhist schools there could be occasions where Buddha's scriptural authority would be cited. However, we must base our argument on reasoning, and the perspective of the contemplative will supersede and invalidate those of the ordinary person because of the contemplative's advanced reasoning. For example, followers of certain tenets accepted by the Sautrantika and Vaibhashika Buddhist schools may cite scriptural sources for the authority of many of their positions. However, if scriptural authority is the only basis on which we can adjudicate, this will create a proliferation of contradictory positions.

Therefore, in Buddhism in general, and particularly in Mahayana Buddhism, it becomes important to distinguish, even within the Buddha's own words, two categories of scriptures. On the one hand there are scriptures that can be accepted at their face value—that is literally, or without qualifications—and there are those that cannot be accepted literally and require further interpretation. Once you accept this hermeneutical distinction, then you will be in a position to reject the literal truth of a scripture, especially when it contradicts your valid experience, even if it is the word of the Buddha himself. What this points to is the critical importance of reasoning and understanding in the Buddhist spiritual approach. The Buddha himself stated in a sutra that people should not accept his words simply out of reverence for him. Rather they must test them against their critical understanding and personal experience, just as a seasoned goldsmith would test the quality of the gold by subjecting it to a rigorous process of cutting, burning, and rubbing.

Shantideva's statement that even the views of those at lower stages of realization are superseded and invalidated by those of the higher ones can be understood as a fact based on our own personal experience. When we examine our own present understanding of such Buddhist topics as impermanence, absence of selfhood of things and events, and so on, and compare this with our past understanding, we find that as our understanding and experience develops it becomes more profound. Because of this, we can say that our present understanding supersedes the realization that we had in the past. So, as we gain new perspectives, new horizons emerge in our experience and understanding of the world.

MEDITATION

Meditate here on the truth of suffering and its origin. The root of suffering is karma, and karma is motivated, and driven, by delusory states such as our afflictions. Investigate: when afflictive emotions arise in us, what does it feel like? The very etymology of "klesha," which means afflictions, implies something that, as it arises in our minds, automatically creates a disturbance. So let us do this brief meditation, investigating how we feel when these troublesome emotions and thoughts, such as anger, hatred, jealousy, and so on, arise in us, and how much our experience of these emotions disturbs us. Concentrate on the destructive aspects of these emotions and thoughts.

4. CRITIQUING THE BUDDHIST REALISTS

PRACTICING WISDOM

Contemplating Impermanence

The Buddha said in sutra that the three realms of existence are impermanent, like lightning in the sky or like mirages. All the phenomena that exist in the three realms of existence, all things and events, have arisen merely through dependence on causes and conditions. Because of this, all things are transient—perishable and impermanent. In particular, the lives of sentient beings are like a torrential river, streaming with force, never stopping still for even a single moment. The lives of all sentient beings are devoid of certainty over any length of time; they are all perishable and transient. These passages point to one of the sixteen characteristics of the four noble truths: the first four are the characteristics of true suffering, and the first of these is impermanence.

As I mentioned above, in the early development of our spiritual path, there are two stages. The first is restraining from negative actions, which are indicators of our deceived states of mind. As an initial counterforce to these, we should contemplate coarse impermanence. And to counteract our deceived states of mind and the misperception that underlies the negative actions, meditation on subtle impermanence is the main antidote and requires us to contemplate deeply the ever-changing, dynamic nature of reality. In this way we can combat the misperceptions, afflictive emotions, and deluded thoughts that persist in the mind.

It is obvious that the end of birth is death, and death is a phenomenon that no one desires. However, to adopt an attitude of denial and to simply avoid thinking about death is not a proper approach. Whether we like it or not, death is a fact of our existence, and there is no point denying its reality. The certainty of death cannot be revoked. It is a phenomenon that we all have to undergo sooner or later. If we compare people who deny death and simply won't think about it with people who cultivate a constant familiarity with the process of facing death directly, we will find a significantly different response in the face of death when it actually strikes. So when we think about the Buddha's emphasis on death and impermanence, we need not have the notion that Buddhism is some kind of pessimistic spiritual path that involves a morbid obsession with death. Rather, we are being encouraged here to make it familiar and to accept it as a natural fact of existence, so that when we encounter the actual moment of death, it does not come as a shock, as something unexpected, unnatural, and utterly overwhelming. If we face our death while we are still healthy, we will be able to maintain our equilibrium and so maintain a degree of calmness when the end nears. In this way, we will safeguard ourselves against unnecessary anxieties that are otherwise associated with death. Slowly, through the spiritual process, if we are fortunate, we will be able to arrive at a point where we will in fact be able to triumph over the anxieties of death, and transcend it.

Combating Our Persistent Discontent

In the scriptures we find mention of four types of *maras,* or obstructive forces, that overwhelm living beings. The first of them is the mara of death, and the basis from which death occurs is our physical and mental aggregates, which constitute the second mara. The continuum of the mental aggregates carries on from one life into another, and the cause of this whole cycle is the various afflictive emotions and thoughts, which constitute the third mara. The key factor that enhances the power of these afflictions is attachment, which is the fourth mara. In Buddhism it is necessary for a spiritual trainee to develop a genuine wish to gain victory over the four maras. Once you develop a genuine desire to overcome them, you will naturally aspire to the path that leads to victory.

In essence, what is involved here for a practitioner is to combat afflictive emotions and thoughts, the root cause of which is the fundamental ignorance—the grasping at things and events as intrinsically real. In order to be successful in this task it is important for the practitioner to engage in a spiritual path that is a combination of the three higher trainings—ethical discipline, concentration, and wisdom.

The first stage of a practice is therefore to maintain an ethically disciplined way of life, centered around the contemplation of impermanence. Unless our clinging to permanence is relaxed, we will not be able to successfully maintain an ethically disciplined way of life. So the crucial point here is to reflect on the transient nature of our existence. We are not talking about impermanence only in terms of death; rather we are referring to subtle impermanence, which is the moment-by-moment, ever-changing nature of all phenomena that reveals how things and events have no self-governing autonomy. All phenomena are governed by causes and conditions. This is especially true of our physical and mental aggregates, governed as they are by karma and afflictions.

So in the case of our conditioned existence, our fundamental misperception, or ignorance, is the governing cause. As long as we remain under the domination of this distorted state, we remain within samsaric bondage, and our existence will be characterized by dissatisfaction and suffering. Therefore this fundamental mis-knowing is the king of all our afflictive emotions and thoughts. Once we recognize this fact, we will realize that as long as we remain under the domination of this powerful ruler, there will be no space in our minds for enduring peace and serenity, and we will develop a genuine desire, from the depths of our heart, to seek freedom and liberation from our bondage to ignorance.

Although we have an innate desire to seek happiness and overcome suffering, we find ourselves within an existence characterized by suffering and only fleeting happiness. Why do we find ourselves in such a state? It is due primarily to our fundamental ignorance. So what is required is to recognize this misknowing as being the root cause of our suffering. What is the process by which this ignorance can be dispelled? Certainly, it is not by simply wishing for it to go away, nor by simply praying for it to happen. Neither is it by remaining in a nonconceptual, neutral state of mind. Only by developing an insight that sees through the illusion created by that distorted state of mind will we be in a position to dispel that ignorance. Therefore, after teaching on impermanence, the Buddha taught the nature of suffering, or unsatisfactoriness, which he then followed by his teaching on selflessness.

So now we have the following four characteristics of suffering. The first is impermanence, the realization of which leads to a deeper awareness of the second characteristic, unsatisfactoriness. The third characteristic is emptiness, and the fourth is the selflessness, or identitylessness, of persons, things, and events. There is a definite sequence to the realization of these four characteristics of suffering, beginning naturally with the understanding of the first characteristic.

It is by developing insight into emptiness that we counter the force of this fundamental ignorance, and this insight must be complemented by the methods of skillful means, such as compassion and the altruistic mind of awakening *(bodhichitta)*. It is only through the combined force of these two factors—wisdom and method—that we will be able to totally eliminate not only the deluded mental states but also the instinctual habits formed by these afflictions. The object of such wisdom or insight is emptiness, and this emptiness is the main topic of Shantideva's ninth chapter.

COMMENTARY

Refuting Appearances

Shantideva has already stated that the tenets and viewpoints of the lower schools of Buddhism are invalidated through reasoning by higher schools such as the Madhyamaka. In order, however, for such arguments to be successful, there must be commonly accepted analogies and examples.

> 4cd. For all employ the same comparisons,
> And the goal, if left unanalyzed, they all accept.

Therefore here in verse 4, when Shantideva speaks of using commonly accepted comparisons and analogies, he is alluding to the fact that, even in everyday convention, certain phenomena are considered unreal or false. For example, there are those phenomena, such as dream objects and mirages, that we cannot find when searching for their reality. Here the Madhyamikas are using analogies that are considered false even in conventional terms to draw attention to the unreality of all phenomena. This draws our attention to the fact that all things and events are ultimately unfindable when we search for their essence.

Although at the initial stage it is through inference that we understand emptiness—through an intellectual process, by using reason, argument, and so on—ultimately this understanding must come at the level of a direct experience. In the scriptures, therefore, inferential knowledge is often compared to a blind person who can only get around with the help of a walking stick. Inferential cognition is not a direct experience; it is an approximation of that experience based on reasoning and critical reflection. However, at the initial stage, it is through inference that we can begin to understand emptiness, the ultimate nature of reality. Contemporary science, such as particle physics, has begun to point toward an understanding of the nature of reality wherein the very notion of objective reality is becoming increasingly untenable. These scientific insights have developed independently of Buddhism. So it seems that through following the conclusion of their own scientific premises, scientists in this field are arriving at a point where they are compelled to entertain the idea of the nonsubstantiality of things and events. Shantideva is stating in this text that there are many grounds, reasons, and arguments that demonstrate the nonsubstantiality of things and events. In contrast, there is not a single premise that can substantiate the belief that things and events possess objective, intrinsic, or autonomous existence.

The fourth verse also alludes to the Realists' objection to the Madhyamaka thesis that things and events lack independent, intrinsic existence. Realists object on the grounds that if this is the case, then how can we maintain that through spiritual practice a person can attain the goal of liberation? The Sautrantika are raising the point here that, according to the Madhyamaka doctrine of emptiness, even causality would be negated.

The Madhyamikas respond to this by saying that the doctrine of emptiness does not deny causality. What is being denied is the validity of causal principles from the viewpoint of ultimate truth. On the conventional level the Madhyamikas argue that they retain the validity of the law of cause and effect. Because it is within the conventional framework—which the Madhyamikas accept without the need to analyze the ultimate nature of things, or without searching for the true referents behind language and concepts—it can simply be accepted as a valid part of the everyday conventional world. Within the framework of relative or conventional truth, they also accept the possibility of attaining, through spiritual practice, the goal of liberation and the state of buddhahood. Therefore, the Madhyamikas insist that their system does not reject causality.

Shantideva continues:

5. When ordinary folk perceive phenomena,
They look on them as real and not illusory.
This, then, is the subject of debate
Where ordinary and meditators differ.

In this verse, Shantideva first presents the Realists' response to the Madhyamikas' defense by having the Realists state, "If you accept the validity of the conventional world, constituted by valid laws of cause and effect, I call that validity real and conclude that cause and effect possesses intrinsic existence. So where is the dispute between you and us? In fact, the dispute may be purely semantic." To this, the Madhyamikas respond, "That is not true. You Realists not only accept the validity of cause and effect at the conventional level, but you believe in the objective, intrinsic reality of these things and events, for you believe that things and events possess some kind of objective, independent status, that they exist in their own right." The Madhyamikas continue, "Although we accept that, to our deluded minds, things and events appear as if they have an autonomous and intrinsic reality and exist independently of our perception, we maintain that this is merely an illusion. We do not ascribe validity to that appearance. We recognize a discrepancy between the way things exist and the way we perceive them to be. That is why there is a dispute between you and us. We do not think this is simply a semantic disagreement."

The next verse begins:

6ab. Forms and so forth, which we sense directly,
Exist by general acclaim, though logic disallows them.

What is common between the Realists and the Madhyamikas is the acceptance of the existence of forms, things, and events. What is being disputed, however, is whether forms and so on exist as they appear to exist. The Realists maintain that not only do forms and so on exist, but also that they exist as they appear to us. They maintain that our perceptions of things and events are valid. As such, they argue, these things and events must possess objective, intrinsic reality.

To this, Madhyamikas say that although it is true that things and events, such as forms, are perceived by valid cognitions such as our sensory perceptions, that does not entail that these perceptions are valid in all aspects. They are valid in perceiving the objects, but they are delusory in perceiving the objects to possess objective, independent, intrinsic existence.

Therefore, according to the Madhyamikas, we can speak of two aspects of perception. From one point of view, it is valid; from another point of view, it is deceptive or deluded. From this understanding we can attribute two aspects to a single event of cognition. Just because we have valid, direct experiences of objects does not mean that these things and events experienced by us possess objective, intrinsic existence. It is in fact this very dispute that lies at the heart of the debate between Bhavaviveka and Chandrakirti that gave rise to the evolution of Madhyamaka-Svatantrika and Madhyamaka-Prasangika as two distinctive schools within the Madhyamaka school. The debate between Bhavaviveka and Chandrakirti centers on the question of whether there are any commonly established objects between the Realists and the Madhyamikas, that is, objects that exist intrinsically and have self-nature.

The verse continues:

> 6cd. They're false, deceiving, like polluted substances
> Regarded in the common view as clean.

The Realists respond: If there is no intrinsic reality or self-nature to things, if things and events do not possess objective, intrinsic existence, why is it that we all perceive it? They argue that there appears to be a common consensus that things are real, at least in so far as our perceptions are concerned. The Madhyamikas reply that a common consensus does not entail that something is true. For example, there seems to be a consensus among ordinary people that the body is pure, while in reality it is polluted and impure, for it is composed of various impure elements. In this way the Madhyamikas defend their negation of intrinsic existence against the objections from the Realists. A key element of their defense is to demonstrate that the belief in intrinsic existence contradicts even our everyday valid experience.

Then, in the seventh verse, the Madhyamikas defend their philosophy of emptiness against objections that are based on citations from the Buddha's scriptures.

7abc. That he might instruct the worldly,
Buddha spoke of "things," but these in truth
Lack even momentariness.

The Realists object to the Madhyamaka view by arguing that the Buddha himself stated in his first public sermon that things and events not only exist, but they also possess defining characteristics such as momentariness, impermanence, and unsatisfactoriness. If forms and so on do not exist inherently, they contend, how can we maintain that they possess these characteristics?

The Madhyamikas respond by saying that the main intention of the Buddha in giving such sermons—talking about the four noble truths and particularly talking about the characteristics of suffering in terms of the four characteristics such as impermanence—was purely to help sentient beings overcome their clinging to permanence and their attachment to samsaric existence. The ultimate aim of these teachings is to lead individuals to the full realization of emptiness. These teachings of the first sermon are, then, skillful means on the path leading to the realization of emptiness. Therefore, the teachings do not contradict the doctrine of emptiness.

Next, Shantideva has the Realists raise a further objection to the Madhyamikas' negation of intrinsic existence. They argue that if things do not exist on the ultimate level, neither would they exist on the relative level. The debate then continues with the Madhyamaka response.

7d. "It's wrong to claim that this is relative!" If so you say,

8. Then know that there's no fault. For momentariness
Is relative for meditators, but for the worldly, absolute.

Were it otherwise, the common view
Could fault our certain insight into corporeal impurity.

The gist of this response is that although, in reality, things and events are momentary and transient, in our everyday view of the world we tend to perceive them as enduring or permanent. However, this is not sufficient to invalidate the fact that things and events are transient and perishable. So there is no inconsistency for the Madhyamika in maintaining the position that things and events are, at the relative level, impermanent, while in the ultimate sense they do not possess this characteristic.

If anything that contradicts our commonsense view is said to be invalid, then the meditative insight into our body as being impure—in the sense of being composed of impure substances such as blood, bones, and flesh—would also become invalid. For in our everyday perceptions we often feel attracted to a beautiful body, experiencing an underlying grasping for it as desirable, perfect, and in some sense pure.

Merit and Rebirth

Next, the Realists level the charge that from the Madhyamaka viewpoint, accumulation of merit becomes impossible.

9ab. "Through a buddha, who is but illusion, how does merit spring?"
As if the Buddha were existing truly.

Here the Realists argue that, according to the Madhyamikas, even the buddhas are illusion-like and therefore not ultimately real. If this is so, they argue, how can we maintain that by venerating objects of refuge, such as the buddhas, we can accumulate merit? To this, the Madhyamikas respond by saying that just as the Realists believe that revering an intrinsically real Buddha accumulates intrinsically real merits, similarly, in our system we can say venerating an illusion-like Buddha accumulates illusion-like merit. There is no inconsistency. So our rejection of intrinsic existence does not negate the possibility of accumulating merit.

The Realists raise another objection:

> 9cd. "But," you ask, "if beings likewise are illusions,
> How, when dying, can they take rebirth?"

They argue that according to the Madhyamaka philosophy of emptiness—which denies true existence and posits existence only in nominal terms—the idea of rebirth becomes untenable, because all sentient beings would also be illusion-like. How can an illusory sentient being take rebirth after death?

To this, the Madhyamikas respond by saying that not only is it possible, but your analogy actually confirms it.

> 10. As long as the conditions are assembled,
> Illusions, likewise, will persist and manifest.
> Why, through simply being more protracted,
> Should sentient beings be regarded as more real?

Even illusion comes into being only in dependence on causes and conditions. Once causes and conditions aggregate, then the result, in this case the illusion, arises. If there is no coming together of causes and conditions, even something like an illusion will not arise. Similarly, as long as there exist within the mindstream the relevant causes and conditions for taking rebirth, this will lead naturally to rebirth after death. So there is no incompatibility between upholding the theory of rebirth on the one hand and maintaining the doctrine of emptiness on the other.

Good and Evil

In verses 11 and 12, the Realists pose the question, "If everything is devoid of intrinsic existence, what grounds are there to distinguish good from evil?"

11. If thus I were to slay or harm a mere mirage,
    Because there is no mind, no sin occurs.
    But beings are possessed of mirage-like minds;
    Sin and merit will, in consequence, arise.

12. Spells and incantations cannot, it is true,
    Give mind to mirages, and so no mind arises.
    But illusions spring from various causes;
    The kinds of mirage, then, are likewise
    various—

13a. A single cause for everything there never was!

If all sentient beings are like mirages or illusions, then there would not be any negative karma accumulated by killing living beings. So, just as by killing magically created illusions we do not accumulate negative karma, according to you Madhyamikas there will not be any negative karma for killing beings, who are like illusions.

Shantideva responds to this objection by stating that there is a significant difference between these two situations. The creations of spells and incantations do not have consciousness. They have no capacity for feeling pain and pleasure; they are mere illusions. So, naturally, slaying a magically created person will not accrue negative karma. In the case of illusion-like sentient beings, however, although they are unreal in that they do not have intrinsic existence, yet they possess the capacity to feel pain and pleasure. They are sentient beings. So slaying an illusion-like sentient being will definitely accrue illusion-like negative karma. There is then a qualitative difference between these two situations.

Samsara and Nirvana

Next, the Madhyamikas answer the accusation that, according to their philosophy of emptiness, no discrimination could be made between samsara and nirvana.

13bcd. "If, ultimately," you will now inquire,
"Everything is said to be nirvana,
Samsara, which is relative, must be the same.

14. "Therefore even buddhahood reverts to the samsaric state.
So why," you ask, "pursue the bodhisattva path?"
As long as there's no cutting of the causal stream,
There is no routing of illusionary appearance.

15ab. But when the causal stream is interrupted,
All illusions, even relative, will cease.

Here, the Realists state that according to the Madhyamikas, all phenomena lack intrinsic existence and that this absence of intrinsic existence is said to be nirvana: If you Madhyamikas call this absence nirvana, then nirvana becomes identical with samsara, because samsara is also devoid of intrinsic existence. If this is so, then according to you Madhyamikas, even samsara becomes nirvana. This cannot be the case, for samsara and nirvana are different. In fact, they are incompatible. Furthermore, if samsara and nirvana are indistinguishable, one will be compelled to accept that even the buddhas remain within the bondage of samsara. Why, then, should spiritual aspirants begin the path in an endeavor to attain the state of buddhahood or liberation when, according to you, samsara and nirvana are ultimately one?

Shantideva responds to this by stating that the Realists have confused the cessation of intrinsic existence, which is a natural nirvana, with nirvana attained through a process of spiritual perfection. Furthermore, cessation is not only an absence of intrinsic existence, it is also a cessation of all our obscurations—both our afflictive emotions and our habitual predispositions. Therefore, we must distinguish between natural nirvana—emptiness—and the meditatively attained nirvana. These are two distinct facts. And as long as the causal stream that leads to a perpetual existence within samsara is not terminated, the individual will remain within samsaric bondage. Once that causal chain is cut, then the individual will not only be in the state of natural nirvana, he or she will also have actualized the nirvana that is freedom from suffering and bondage.

The point being made here by the Realists is that without accepting the intrinsic and objective reality of things, there would be no causality, no way that phenomena could function. To all of these objections, the Madhyamikas respond by stating that, although they maintain that all things and events are illusion-like in that they do not have intrinsic, independent reality, they do accept the validity of causality and other functions of the relative world. The Madhyamikas state that the reality of the conventional world is not destroyed by their logic of emptiness but is left completely intact.

So, in the aftermath of negating intrinsic existence, what is crucial is to be able to maintain the validity of the world of conventional truth. If we are able to do this, we will arrive at the true "Middle Way," a position free from the extremes of absolutism and nihilism. And because this position does not negate the reality and validity of the conventional world, it retains all functionality, such as cause and effect, subject and object, and so on. Once we arrive at this viewpoint, then we have definitely earned the hallmark of being a person within the true Middle Way. Otherwise, our philosophical position falls into one of the two extremes. Either it negates the reality of the conventional world and descends further and further into a nihilistic position, or it swings to the other extreme and upholds some form of absolutism, grasping for something absolute or eternal. According to Shantideva and the Madhyamikas, it is crucial for a spiritual trainee to be able to maintain the balance of the Middle Way position.

MEDITATION

Take a moment now to do another brief meditation. The theme of this meditation is subtle impermanence. First, reflect upon your own body, particularly on the circulation of blood. How does the heart pump the blood? If you reflect on that, you experience that there is something dynamic about your body; it never remains in a static state. And if you reflect upon external objects, you observe the same phenomenon. For example, when you see a historic building, you might reflect, "This house is several centuries old." Even while maintaining its continuum in time, however, the house has been going through a process of moment-to-moment change all the while.

Reflect upon this subtle impermanence, this dynamic process, this momentary, ever-changing nature of phenomena. This is not confined to external objects; it extends also to our mindstream. Although there is a continuum, if we reflect upon individual instances of our cognitive events—the emotions, thoughts, and mental states that we have—we will find that they are all momentarily changing. They never remain still. So reflect upon this moment-to-moment, changing, and dynamic nature of internal and external phenomena. This, in brief, is how you can contemplate the subtle impermanence of all things and events.

5. THE MIND-ONLY VIEWPOINT

COMMENTARY

The External World

We are now at the section that is specifically concerned with refuting the views of the Mind-Only, or *Chittamatra,* school. First, Shantideva has the Mind-Only school present its theses, which are then followed by his refutations from the Madhyamaka position. In the text the Mind-Only view is stated as a question:

15cd. "If that which is deceived does not exist,
What is it," you ask, "that sees illusion?"

The objection is that if, as the Madhyamikas contend, all phenomena are like illusions, then conceptions, perceptions, and consciousness must also be illusion-like. If this is so, they ask, what is it that perceives the illusions?

This objection of the Mind-Only school is refuted in various ways by the Madhyamikas. One refutation is based on drawing parallels. Among the four Buddhist schools of thought, there are two Hinayana schools—Sautrantika and Vaibhashika—and two Mahayana schools—Chittamatra and Madhyamaka. Both Mahayana schools accept the selflessness of phenomena. However, their understanding of what constitutes the meaning of this selflessness differs between the Mind-Only school and the Middle Way school.

The Mind-Only school understands reality in terms of what are known as the three natures. These are the *dependent nature,* the *imputed nature,* and the *thoroughly established* or *ultimate nature*. It is within this framework that the Mind-Only speaks of the selflessness of phenomena. The self, or the identity to be negated, in their understanding of the selflessness of phenomena, pertains primarily to the way in which language and concepts relate to their referents, or objects. For example, they argue that forms or everyday objects such as vases, pillars, and tables do not exist in their own right as the basis for terms. In this view, all external phenomena are, in the final analysis, projections of the mind—they are ultimately extensions of the mind. In this sense, the Mind-Only school rejects the reality of the external world. They contend that if we carefully examine everyday objects such as vases and tables, they appear to us to have some kind of independent status—as if they exist "out there"—while in reality, everyday objects are nothing but extensions of our mind. They are projections, or constructions, arising from within our mind, and they do not have an independent, objective reality outside. Once you appreciate the lack of reality of the external world in this way, there is certainly a marked decrease in your tendency to grasp onto the perceived solidity of the external world. So the central thesis of the Mind-Only school—which is being refuted by Shantideva—is that the external world is illusory, and the perceptions we have of external objects are projections constructed by the mind due to predispositions that are deeply embedded in the mind.

In the next verse, Shantideva states that, according to the Mind-Only school, even the reality of the external world cannot be maintained.

16. But, if for you, these same illusions have no being,
What, indeed, remains to be perceived?

If objects have another mode of being,
That very mode is but the mind itself.

By upholding that external objects do not really exist and that they are mere projections of the mind, the Mind-Only school is accepting a certain degree of discrepancy between our perceptions and the reality of the external world. If this is so, the Madhyamikas argue, then the Mind-Only already accepts the illusion-like nature of reality at least in so far as the external world is concerned. They would therefore have to accept that external objects do not possess true, or intrinsic, existence—they have no real ontological status. Even the Mind-Only would have to deny the reality of illusion itself.

The Self-Cognizing Mind

The Mind-Only may respond to this by stating that although external objects do not exist the way we perceive them—as enjoying autonomous, objective reality—this does not entail that they do not exist as expressions of the mind. Although they do not exist independently, they can be said to exist as mental phenomena. That is a feasible defense by the Mind-Only school. However, this is contested by the Madhyamikas in the next verse:

17. But if the mirage is the mind itself,
What, then, is perceived by what?
The Guardian of the World himself has said
That mind cannot be seen by mind.

They argue that if the mirage-like external objects are mere extensions of the mind, then in reality they are part of the mind. If this is so, the Mind-Only will be compelled to maintain that, when mind perceives external objects, what is happening is that the mind is perceiving mind. How can we coherently speak of subjects and objects in a situation where, after all, there is nothing but mind itself?

In the next two lines, Shantideva cites a sutra in which the Buddha states that no matter how sharp a blade is, it cannot cut itself.

18. In just the same way, he has said,
The sword's edge cannot cut the sword.
"But," you say, "it's like the flame
That perfectly illuminates itself."

Similarly, a consciousness can never perceive itself. He is stating that the concept of self-cognizing consciousness is untenable. The Mind-Only school responds to this critique by defending that it is possible to conceive a mind cognizing itself. They use the analogy of a lamp. Just as a lamp can illuminate other objects because its nature is self-luminous, the consciousness too cognizes other objects because it is self-cognizing. The Madhyamikas do not accept this explanation and respond:

19ab. The flame, in fact, can never light itself.
And why? Because the darkness never dims it!

The Mind-Only response is to invoke another analogy:

19cd. "The blueness of a blue thing," you will say,
"Depends, unlike a crystal, on no other thing.

20ab. "Likewise some perceptions
Rise from other things, while some do not."

They argue that we can differentiate two different types of blue. For example, if a clear crystal is placed on a blue cloth, it will assume a bluish color. However, this blueness is derived from other factors—the presence of the blue cloth underneath it. In contrast, there are blue precious stones in which the blueness is not derived from other factors. So, in the second instance, the quality of blueness is an essential property, while in the first, it is contingent. Similarly, they argue, there are two principal kinds of cognitive events. The first is our sensory perceptions, which take on external objects. The second kind do not take on external objects but perceive cognition itself. So the Mind-Only school distinguishes between self-cognizers and cognizers of other objects. This defense by the Mind-Only is refuted by Shantideva:

20cd. But what is blue has never of itself imposed
A blueness on its non-blue self.

He argues that there is no quality of blueness that is not dependent on other factors. Blueness is a quality of a thing, and all things and events must depend on other causes and conditions for their coming into being. Just as the blueness of the crystal is dependent on other factors, the blueness of lapis lazuli is also dependent on other conditions. Shantideva continues:

21. The phrase "the lamp illuminates itself"
The mind can know and formulate.
But what is there to know and say
That "mind is self-illuminating"?

22. The mind, indeed, is never seen by anyone,
And therefore, whether it can know or cannot
know itself,
Just like the beauty of a barren woman's daughter,
This merely forms the subject of a pointless
conversation.

The Mind-Only has to admit that a lamp does not illuminate itself, for if this were the case, we would be compelled to maintain that darkness too conceals itself. Yet, without subscribing to the view that a lamp is self-illuminating, we can still maintain that the lamp is illuminating. And just as a lamp is not self-illuminating, the Madhyamikas argue, then the fact that cognitions do not cognize themselves does not entail that cognitions are not by their very nature cognizing.

Shantideva argues that even the very act of illumination is dependent on other factors—there cannot be illumination without something that is illuminated. Similarly, there cannot be a cognition without an object. It would be like speaking about the daughter of a barren woman!

However, the Mind-Only school presents an argument to prove the self-knowing, or apperceptive, quality of perception:

23ab. "But if," you ask, "the mind is not self-knowing,
How does it remember what it knew?"

Generally speaking, the criterion by which we determine whether something exists is whether it can be established by a valid cognition. If any thing or event can be established by a valid cognition, it can be said to exist. So the reality of a phenomenon depends on the validity of the perception or cognition. Yet, the validity of the cognition depends in turn upon its relation to reality; so there is a relationship of mutual dependence between cognitions and their objects. Without an object there cannot be a subject, and no cognition or awareness.

However, the Mind-Only school does not accept this mutual dependence between cognition and its object. According to their view, some privileged status is accorded to consciousness, or subject, because the subjective experience certifies the reality of the objects. However, the reality of the subject must also be certified. In other words, the cognition or subject too must be cognized. If every cognition requires another instance of cognition for its establishment, then the chain would extend *ad infinitum*. Therefore, the Mind-Only argues, we have to maintain that cognition must necessarily cognize itself; there must be a self-knowing faculty to our cognitive events that allows our cognitions to perceive themselves.

For these reasons, the Mind-Only school accepts a self-cognizing faculty of consciousness *(rang rik)*. Their argument is based upon the premise of recollection, that when we are remembering, we are not only remembering the object but also recalling our perception of that object. This indicates, according to them, that when we initially perceived that object, there must have been a further faculty that registered our experience. The Mind-Only argues that, just as in ordinary language we cannot speak of recollection without a prior perception of an object or an event, similarly, we cannot speak of the recollection of an experience without a prior perception of that experience. Thus, they conclude, there must have been a self-perceiving awareness at the time we initially perceived the object.

Shantideva gives an alternative account of recollection:

> 23cd. We say that like the poison of the water rat,
> It's from the link with outer things that memory occurs.

From the viewpoint of the Madhyamika, equal power is given to both subject and object, because the subject and object are mutually dependent. That is to say, each depends on the other and derives its validity on the basis of the other. The Madhyamika therefore does not accord any privileged status to the consciousness.

Khunu Lama Rinpoche states that when you perceive, say, a blue color through sensory perception and later recollect your perception, the very act of recollecting the object is mixed with the recollection of the perception. Recollection of an object can never arise independently of the experience of that object. It is because of this that the subjective experience is also recalled when we recall the object. There is no need to posit an independent, self-perceiving faculty to account for recollection.

Then the Mind-Only school presents another argument in their defense of self-cognition.

> 24. "In certain cases," you will say, "the mind
> Can see the minds of others, how then not itself?"

But through the application of a magic balm,
The eye may see the treasure, but the salve it does
not see.

They argue that, through deep meditative absorption, it is possible for certain individuals to acquire a clairvoyance that allows them to perceive other people's minds. The mind must therefore have the capacity to perceive what is even closer and more familiar—itself.

Madhyamikas respond to this with a different analogy. They argue that although the use of magical powers and substances may make it possible for individuals to perceive objects buried beneath the ground, that still does not provide that person's eye with the power to perceive itself. Similarly, they argue, just because a mind can perceive others' minds does not entail that it can also perceive itself.

According to the Mind-Only school, if we do not accept this faculty of self-cognition, we deprive ourselves of the grounds to establish the validity of consciousness. So Shantideva reiterates that we are not negating sights, sounds, and cognitions:

25. It's not indeed our object to disprove
Experiences of sight or sound or knowing.
Our aim is here to undermine the cause of sorrow:
The thought that such phenomena have true
existence.

We are negating our misperception of the things we see, hear, and know as being intrinsically real, for this misperception is the root cause of our suffering.

Seeing Through Self-Grasping

To understand how this fundamental ignorance—grasping at intrinsic existence—lies at the root of our bondage, it is important to have some understanding of the psychological and phenomenological process entailed when afflictions arise within us.

When we experience these negative emotions arising, such as anger, hatred, and attachment, we should examine how the objects of our emotions appear to us, that is, how we perceive them. In our normal interactions with the world, we perceive things as enjoying an objective, independent status, existing "out there"; this is because we tend to relate to the world through our dualistic perceptions. We tend to go along with our perceptions, grasping at the images they present to us, as if they possess some objective, intrinsic reality. This is especially true when we are in the midst of strong emotions.

For example, when we are experiencing a strong desire for someone or something, at that instant the object of our attraction appears as if it is one hundred percent perfect and desirable. That desirability appears to exist independently of our perception. Similarly, when we experience intense anger or hatred, the object of our anger appears as if it actually possesses this hatefulness independently of our perception. There is a tendency in us to look at things in black-and-white terms when caught up in strong emotions, perceiving things to be either one hundred percent good or one hundred percent bad. During these occasions, we should really try to discern how we are actually relating to the world, and how our misperception of things and events as intrinsically real distorts our interactions with the world around us.

When we carefully analyze these intense emotions, such as anger, attachment, and jealousy, we will discover within their causal processes a strong sense of "I" or self at the core. Feelings such as "I don't want this," "I am repulsed by it," or "I feel drawn to it," underlie our emotional experience. How are we to relate to and counter this strong sense of "I"? Analysis is one step. Another step in countering these afflictions is to try to reduce the force of our grasping at the concreteness of the object of our emotions.

Take the example of your attitude toward a valued possession, like your car, or your watch. If you have strong attachment to watches, for instance, try to recall how you reacted to your watch before you bought it—when it was still in the shop, on the shelf—and compare your feelings about it after you bought it. Now that it is "yours," the watch becomes associated with your ego-consciousness, "I am." In the shop, there was certainly an attraction toward it, but there was less association with your sense of self because it did not "belong" to you. So, here we can observe how we feel differently about the same object.

Generally speaking, emotions such as anger and attachment come in different degrees. These degrees correspond to the amount of grasping onto a sense of self or the thought, "I am." At a gross level we tend to conceive the self as an entity independent of our body and mind, in the manner of a controller, possessing some kind of self-sufficient, autonomous reality. Grasping at this sense of self is quite instinctual. For example, if it were necessary and we felt we would benefit, we would find it perfectly acceptable to use medical science to have a heart transplant or have a limb amputated. Were it possible, we would be willing to even exchange our body for a different one if this contributed to our well-being. Similarly, if we felt we would be better off for the exchange—might we also be prepared to exchange even our mind? Such a willingness indicates that we do have a belief in a sense of a self that is quite independent of our body and mind. What Shantideva has been demonstrating here in the text is the absence of such a self. According to him, the self, or person, exists only on the basis of the aggregates. Apart from the body and mind, there is no such entity called the "self."

The point of this is that once you reflect on this absence of selfhood, there will definitely be a corresponding decrease in your grasping at such a self, thus leading to a marked loosening of your grip on a rigid sense of a self or ego. I mentioned above that if you view all external objects as projections of the mind—as something created by your own deluded mind—this brings a marked decrease in your attachment toward external objects. In the same manner, as you begin to recognize the absence of this independent, autonomous self, your instinctive grasping at such a self will begin to loosen.

Illusion and Mind

Next Shantideva presents another thesis of the Mind-Only school.

> 26. "Illusions are not other than the mind," you say,
> And yet you also claim that they are not the same.
> But must they not be different if the mind is real?
> And how can mind be real if there's no difference?

This is the assertion that an illusion is neither different from the mind nor identical to it—illusion is not the mind itself. Since illusion is neither identical nor separate, it must be a projection of the mind.

Shantideva argues that if illusion exists externally, how can the Mind-Only assert that it is a mere projection of the mind? If, on the other hand, illusion does not possess any external reality, then the illusion becomes a mere creation of the mind, in which case, how can the Mind-Only maintain that everyday objects like forms, tables, and vases actually exist? They cannot be real in any sense from the Mind-Only point of view.

However, the Mind-Only adherents maintain that although external objects are like mirages and do not exist, they can still be observed.

> 27. "A mirage may be known," you say, "though lacking true existence."
> The knower is the same: it knows but is a mirage.
> "But what supports samsara must be real," you say,
> "Or else samsara is like empty space."

Shantideva responds that likewise, although mind does not exist from the perspective of ultimate truth, we can still maintain that mind is observable. To this, the Mind-Only school replies that cyclic existence must have some objective, substantial basis in reality; otherwise it would be like the empty space, which for them is a mere conceptual abstraction. The Mind-Only, while viewing space as an abstract entity, still maintain that it must have some substantial basis in reality. Shantideva then reiterates that, from the Mind-Only view, only mind enjoys real existence.

28. But how could the unreal proceed to function,
Even if it rests on something real?
This mind of yours is isolated and alone,
Alone, in solitude, and unaccompanied.

29. If the mind indeed is free of objects,
All beings must be buddhas, thus gone and enlightened.
Therefore what utility or purpose can there be
In saying thus, that there is "only mind?"

Therefore the Mind-Only are compelled by their own logic to accept that mind exists independently of all objects for, ultimately, it is only the mind that exists. If this is so, then this resembles the *dharmakaya* state, in which all thought processes of the external world have been dissolved and no dualistic appearances remain.

In the end, the Mind-Only will have to accept that since nothing exists apart from mind, the mind must be free of all dualistic elaborations. This is because all forms of duality are mere illusions and therefore do not exist. This further implies that all sentient beings, possessing minds as they do, are buddhas, fully enlightened and free of delusions and dualistic perceptions. In this way, Shantideva demonstrates that the Mind-Only school's view results in absurd conclusions.

The Middle Way Approach

Now Shantideva begins the discussion of the necessity of the Middle Way path. First, he presents an objection to the Madhyamaka position on the emptiness of intrinsic existence:

30. Even if we know that all is like illusion,
How will this dispel afflictive passion?

Magicians may indeed desire
The mirage-women they themselves create.

Shantideva responds to this criticism in the following verse:

31. The reason is they have not rid themselves
Of habits of desiring objects of perception;
And when they gaze upon such things,
Their aptitude for emptiness is weak indeed.

He agrees it is true that even the magician—as the creator of an illusory woman—sometimes has lustful feelings, even though he knows that she is a mere illusion. Shantideva says this is due to his habitual inclinations and patterns of thought. Similarly, even after understanding the illusion-like, empty nature of phenomena, we too have the habitual tendency to grasp at things and events as if they were intrinsically real. This is because of instinctual habits formed over many lifetimes.

When we speak of seeds or propensities here, it is critical to recognize that there are primarily two different types. The first are propensities or imprints in the form of potential, which can manifest later in consciousness in more overt forms. The other types are not so much potentials as tendencies, which remain as habitual patterns, influencing our perceptions and attitudes.

Shantideva states that by developing constant familiarity with our insight into emptiness, we gradually overcome the effects of these powerful habitual instincts. Once we have gained deep insight into emptiness—negating grasping to all extremes—then all dualistic tendencies and grasping will cease. Then, through constant familiarity and development of that profound insight, we gradually overcome even the habitual inclination to grasp at intrinsic existence.

What is essential is for us to get at the root and realize subtle emptiness, as this negates all degrees of substantial and intrinsic reality. It is vital that our realization of emptiness does not remain incomplete, like the understanding of the Mind-Only school. That understanding negates the reality of the external world, but it still asserts that mind, or consciousness, enjoys some kind of absolute reality. There is thus still a powerful basis for grasping, for our understanding of emptiness has not reached its full scope.

Compared to the Mind-Only position, the Svatantrika-Madhyamaka school takes a further step by asserting that neither mind nor external objects possess substantial existence. However, they still accept some subtle form of intrinsic reality of both mind and its object, thus their understanding of emptiness is not final either.

In the case of the Prasangika-Madhyamaka understanding of emptiness, since all intrinsic reality has been negated, this deep insight into emptiness is complete and final and demolishes all tendencies for grasping at anything as absolute. This then is the true understanding of emptiness that we must cultivate.

Shantideva issues a caution for us in the next verse.

32. By training in this aptitude for emptiness,
The habit to perceive substantiality will fade.
By training in the view that all lacks entity,
This view itself will also disappear.

What is emphasized here is to be critically aware of the danger of reifying emptiness itself. You might conclude that although all things and events are empty of intrinsic existence, emptiness itself is absolute. Shantideva states that when our view of emptiness is perfect, even the tendency to reify emptiness and conceive it as some kind of an absolute will be dispelled. Although there is a slight difference in the interpretation of this point between Khenpo Künpal and Minyak Künsö's commentaries, ultimately they converge on the same point—the need to develop a complete realization of emptiness so that it frees us from grasping even emptiness as truly existent.

In the next two verses, Shantideva shows that, by meditating on emptiness, we can attain a nonconceptual state.

33. "There is nothing"—when this is asserted,
No "thing" is there to be examined.
For how can nothing, lacking all support,
Remain before the mind as something present?

34. When real and nonreal both
Are absent from before the mind,
Nothing else remains for mind to do
But rest in perfect peace, from concepts free.

Shantideva states that, as a Madhyamika, he accepts the validity of all conventionalities—such as the law of cause and effect and the possibility of attaining liberation—within the relative framework. Within their framework of true existence of things and events, realists also speak of the path and the possibility of attaining full liberation. Shantideva argues that, while maintaining that ultimately all things are unreal and do not enjoy intrinsic existence, we can still speak coherently of the possibility of attaining buddhahood. He makes this point in the following verses:

35. As the wishing jewel and tree of miracles
Fulfill and satisfy all hopes and wishes,
Likewise, through their prayers for those who might be trained,
Victorious ones appear within the world.

36. The healing shrine of the garuda,
Even when its builder was long dead,
Continued even ages thence
To remedy and soothe all plagues and venom.

37. Likewise, though the bodhisattva has transcended sorrow,
By virtue of his actions for the sake of buddhahood,

The shrines of buddha forms appear and manifest,
Enacting and fulfilling every deed.

Then Shantideva has his adversary raise the question:

38ab. "But how," you ask, "can offerings made
To beings freed from all discursiveness give fruit?"

And he answers:

38cd. It's said that whether buddhas live or pass beyond,
The offerings made to them have equal merit.

39. Whether you assert the relative or ultimate,
The scriptures say that merit will result.
Merits will be gained regardless
Of the Buddha's true or relative existence.

MEDITATION

Now do a brief meditation. Imagine you are experiencing an intense emotion, such as anger or attachment, toward someone. Then imagine how, caught up in the emotion, you would respond in a scenario involving that person. Analyze how you relate to the object of your anger or attachment, and compare this with how you relate to people in your normal state of mind. Look at the differences between these two scenarios and compare them. This way, you will learn to recognize the psychological process involved in a forceful affliction, such as anger, and appreciate how grasping at some reified qualities of the person lies at the root of an afflictive emotions.

6. THE AUTHENTICITY OF THE MAHAYANA

PRACTICING WISDOM

Creating the Causes for Happiness

Chandrakirti states in his *Supplement to the Middle Way* that the entire world of sentient beings and their environments is a result of causes and conditions. He is referring specifically to the causes and conditions that constitute the karma of sentient beings. Each individual comes into being and each disintegrates and ceases to exist, and if we trace the continuum of the causes and conditions themselves, we find that basically it comes down to karma, whether positive or negative. Karma itself is rooted in intention and motivation, so in effect it all comes down to the individual's state of mind. From a disciplined and calm state of mind, desirable and positive consequences follow, and from an undisciplined, negative motivation and state of mind, undesirable experiences of pain and suffering follow. Because of this, the Buddha stated in various sutras that the mind is the creator of all sentient beings and of samsara; this applies also to nirvana. So, in a sense, the mind is the creator of both samsara and nirvana.

All individuals are equal in that every one of us instinctively seeks happiness and avoids suffering. The way to fulfill this aspiration is through seeking out the actual causes and conditions that develop and enhance our happiness and eliminating the factors that cause suffering and pain. This is the true essence of Dharma practice.

The immediate state of our mind—happy, irritated, or otherwise—depends of course on many factors, including physical conditions such as exhaustion or relaxation. However, many of our thought processes do not depend primarily on physiological conditions. So, ultimately it is by bringing about an internal transformation that we can effect the desired change in our state of mind.

When we speak of the mind or consciousness, we should not have the notion that we are talking about a monolithic entity. Just as there are many different types of matter, there are also many different types of consciousness comprising our inner world; there are diverse dispositions, mental states, thought processes, and so on. In the case of external, material objects, we recognize that some are beneficial and some are harmful, and based on our discrimination, we avoid contact with harmful substances while utilizing and developing the potential of the positive ones. Similarly, in the case of our inner world—by choosing from among the variety of our mental states—we can enhance the capacity and potential of those states of mind that will not only create an immediate sense of serenity, but will also give rise to happier, more positive, and calmer states of mind in the future.

Certain kinds of thoughts and emotions, when they arise, immediately cause a disturbance, afflicting our mind and creating a negative atmosphere. Even among those thoughts and emotions that initially provide a sense of happiness or pleasure, some may in the long run actually be destructive. It is therefore crucial to correctly distinguish between mental states that are harmful and those that are truly beneficial.

Among those that are beneficial, we must distinguish between long-term and short-term beneficial effects. When these two criteria come into conflict, we should regard those with long-term consequences as more important. Some states of mind initially create irritation, unhappiness, or a lack of joy. However, by staying calm and facing them—going through the various challenges they provide—it is possible for these situations to eventually produce happier and more stable states of mind. So it is important to be able to compare long-term and short-term consequences. With such discernment we can develop those positive states of mind that produce long-term beneficial effects.

When we speak of which actions and states of mind need to be enhanced and which need to be discarded, we must choose and pursue the task intelligently. The faculty that generates this discernment is called *discriminating awareness*. This is, in fact, one of the distinguishing features of being human. Although all sentient beings are equal in having the instinctive wish to be happy and overcome suffering, human beings have a greater capacity to think in terms of long-term and short-term consequences. Because of this, human beings have a greater imaginative faculty and therefore a greater capacity to fulfill their aspiration to seek happiness and to avoid suffering.

Among the various types of discriminating awareness, the most important is the one that penetrates the ultimate nature of reality—the realization of emptiness. There are many factors we can use to develop this wisdom, including, most importantly, the study of the scriptures that outline the philosophy of emptiness. This is what we are doing here in this book.

Two Intellectual Cultures

Generally speaking, we can say that in the East philosophers have paid more attention to understanding the nature of the internal world. This is particularly the case within the Buddhist tradition. The Western scientific tradition generally seems to place greater emphasis on the investigation of the external world. Because of this we can speak of the East and the West in terms of two distinct intellectual cultures, where the emphasis differs regarding the exploration of the internal and external worlds. As human beings, we need both.

In the East, although there is science and technology, they are not fully developed and remain in an early stage. Similarly, in the West there are various disciplines of psychology, but because the intellectual culture emphasizes the exploration of the external world, the discipline of psychology remains in an early stage. Therefore, just as we need more scientific and technological development in the East, in the West there is a need to further develop the understanding of mind, consciousness, and self.

Because of this, there are quite a few Westerners who take an academic interest in Eastern religions. This interest stems not so much from seeking a personal spiritual path, but rather as an investigation of something that is an object of intellectual curiosity. I think this is very healthy, because by studying others' viewpoints, it is possible for us to discover new and refreshing perspectives on the world—including our own life.

COMMENTARY

Mahayana Authenticity and Emptiness

We continue now with our root text, starting from verse 40. It is the beginning of a subsection in which Shantideva talks about the necessity of realizing emptiness even to gain liberation from samsaric existence as opposed to full enlightenment. With regard to the reading of these verses, the two Tibetan commentaries differ, and this difference in turn leads to a divergence in the way the root text is divided into sections.

Khenpo Künpal states in his commentary that from this point onward, the main emphasis is to prove the validity or authenticity of the Mahayana scriptures. In contrast, Minyak Künsö's commentary says that the emphasis is on proving the thesis that, even in order to gain liberation from samsara, the realization of emptiness is indispensable. Given that they perceive different points of emphasis, there will of course also be differences of interpretation.

First, an opening argument is presented concerning the Madhyamaka school's great emphasis on the realization of emptiness. Here Shantideva has his opponent ask, "since it is possible to attain liberation from samsara by meditating on and understanding the nature of the four noble truths, what need is there to realize emptiness?"

40. "We're freed," you say, "through seeing the
 [four] truths—
 What use is it to us, this view of emptiness?"
 But as the scriptures have themselves proclaimed,
 Without it there is no enlightenment.

Shantideva responds to this by arguing that in the scriptures, the Buddha himself has stated that without the path of emptiness, there is no possibility of even attaining freedom from cyclic existence. The scriptures he is referring to here are the Mahayana perfection of wisdom *(prajnaparamita)* sutras.

In the perfection of wisdom sutras, the Buddha states that it is not possible to gain freedom while we are grasping onto phenomena as truly existent. He states that even to attain nirvana, or cessation of suffering, realization of emptiness is essential. This argument, however, is based on the assumption that the Mahayana scriptures are authentic teachings of the Buddha.

Other Buddhist traditions, such as the Hinayana, dispute the authenticity of Mahayana scriptures as being Buddha's words. Shantideva therefore places great emphasis on demonstrating that Mahayana scriptures are authentic teachings of the Buddha. So, in the next verse, Shantideva has his opponent question the very authenticity of the Mahayana scriptures.

41. You say the Mahayana has no certainty.
 But how do you substantiate your own tradition?
 "Because it is accepted by both parties," you will say.
 But at the outset, you yourselves lacked proof.

Shantideva responds by asking the question, "But how do you substantiate your own tradition?" The Madhyamikas are raising the point here that even the scriptures that the Hinayana consider to be valid cannot be authenticated right from the start. The opponents respond to this by pointing out that in the case of the Hinayana scriptures, both parties accept their validity, whereas in the case of the Mahayana scriptures, the Hinayanist disputes its validity. The Madhyamikas respond by stating that this shows that the authenticity of Hinayana scriptures is not self-evident, because they have not been authenticated from the outset either. That is to say, surely the Hinayana must have some grounds upon which they have accepted their scripture's validity.

Likewise, Shantideva continues in the next verse, if you consider the reasons why I trust the Mahayana scriptures as valid, then you too will be compelled to accept their validity.

> 42. The reasons why you trust in your tradition
> May likewise be applied to Mahayana.
> Moreover, if accord between two parties shows
> the truth,
> The Vedas and rest are also true.

If you still persist with your argument that because both parties—Hinayana and Mahayana—are in accord in accepting the validity of the Hinayana scriptures, and therefore they can be considered valid and authentic, then in line with this reasoning, you would also have to accept the truth of, say, the Vedic teachings, because there will always be two parties who uphold their authenticity.

Shantideva continues in the next verse that if, just because there are people who contest the validity and authenticity of the Mahayana scriptures, this implies sufficient reason to question their validity, then we will have to question the validity of the Hinayana scriptures also.

43. "Mahayana is at fault," you say, "because it is
contested."
But by non-Buddhists are your scriptures also
questioned,
While other Buddhist schools impugn and spurn them.
Therefore, your tradition you must now abandon.

Surely there will always be people, both Buddhist and non-Buddhist, who will dispute the validity of certain Hinayana scriptures. Just because it is disputed by some individuals does not mean that it is untrustworthy. In short, Shantideva argues that whatever grounds the Hinayanist employs to prove the authenticity of the Hinayana scriptures can equally be applied to the Mahayana teachings. Through these arguments, Shantideva attempts to prove the authenticity of the Mahayana scriptures.

Other arguments can also be made to demonstrate the validity of the Mahayana scriptures. For instance, Nagarjuna states that if the Mahayana teachings—a system that explains various levels, grounds, and spiritual paths—did not exist, then we would not be able to attain full enlightenment. Simply engaging in the path of the thirty-seven aspects of the path to enlightenment, as taught in the Hinayana teachings, is not sufficient. This path of the thirty-seven aspects is common to all three levels of objective—the attainments of hearers *(shravaka arhat)* and of solitary realizers *(pratyekabuddha arhat)* and buddhahood. If there exists a major difference at the fruition level, then naturally we would expect a major difference at the causal level as well. Nagarjuna argues it is only by relying on the teachings in the Mahayana scriptures that we can actually establish the validity of the Buddha's path in general.

Buddhahood and the Three Kayas

According to the Hinayana sutras, Buddha Shakyamuni remained as Prince Siddhartha until the age of twenty-nine. Later, as a result of engaging in six years of meditative practices, based on adopting a monastic way of life, he become fully enlightened around the age of thirty-five. During the next forty-five years, following his full enlightenment, the Buddha worked to fulfill the aspirations of sentient beings. Then at Kushinagara, at the age of eighty, the Buddha entered into *parinirvana.* According to the Hinayana scriptures, the Buddha at that point disappeared into nothingness, and the continuity of his consciousness ceased to exist. If that were the case, we would have to accept that after accumulating merit and wisdom for three innumerable eons, the fulfillment was working for other sentient beings for a mere forty-five years! Rather than being in a totally nonexistent state where the continuum of consciousness has ceased—that is, nirvana—I would personally prefer to have a continuum of consciousness, even if this meant remaining in cyclic existence.

The Mahayana scriptures, by contrast, maintain that Prince Siddhartha, who became fully enlightened, was a *nirmanakaya*—the buddha body of perfect emanation—and was already fully enlightened. Such a being, in its natural embodiment, is *dharmakaya,* the buddha body of reality. From within that sphere, it assumes *sambhogakaya*, the buddha body of perfect resource, from which a buddha assumes various physical embodiments. From one point of view, this conception of buddhahood may seem inconceivable. From another point of view, however, there is a much greater coherence if we correlate the description of buddhahood—its features, qualities, and so on, as described in the Mahayana literature—with the complexity of the causal conditions that give rise to the fully enlightened state. I think this notion of buddhahood has much greater coherence and makes more sense than the state of nonexistence described in the Hinayana scriptures.

The Effects of Wisdom

The Buddha states in the sutras that an effect comes into being in correspondence with its cause. This is the general principle of causality. Ignorance, as a cause, compels the individual to engage in various acts, both negative and positive. These acts again engender multiple effects, such as taking rebirth in the various realms of existence. Even within one single rebirth, there are multiple effects, such as the environment into which a person is born. There is tremendous diversity among sentient beings, and this is due to the diversity of the causes and conditions that create them. All these different forms of existence are replete with suffering. Thus, if a cause like the ignorant mind can bring such a diversity of effects, it is conceivable that the causes of wisdom will lead to multiple and diverse results also. If, however, we were to maintain that the only effect of wisdom is the attainment of full enlightenment with no subsequent fulfillment of the welfare of other sentient beings, then it seems to suggest that ignorance is a more powerful cause, because it can give rise to such diverse effects. This does not make much sense!

Origins of the Mahayana Scriptures

Most importantly, the principle of the four noble truths is accepted by all schools of Buddhism. These teachings on the four noble truths lay down the foundation of the entire Buddhist path. As I mentioned above, in order to develop a full understanding of the third truth, cessation, we need to rely on the teachings of the Mahayana scriptures. Without the detailed explanations found in the Mahayana scriptures, full understanding of the truth of cessation cannot arise.

We might feel that many of the Hinayana scriptures, such as those recorded in Pali, are universally accepted as authentic expressions of the Buddha, whereas the Mahayana scriptures are not universally accepted. They are not among the teachings canonized at the three councils that took place after the Buddha's death. One could become suspicious. To this concern, Bhavaviveka responds in his *Blaze of Reasoning (Tarkajvala)* that the Mahayana scriptures were collected and compiled by bodhisattvas such as Vajrapani.

Many of the Hinayana scriptures derive from public discourses, whereas Mahayana scriptures were not taught openly in public. I personally feel, therefore, that these scriptures cannot be judged purely in terms of conventional, historical criteria. Their evolution may need to be understood more in terms of what could be called a mystical perspective. For example, many scriptures belonging to the Vajrayana tradition were taught by the Buddha while assuming the form and identity of the meditational deities. Similarly, many scriptures attributed to the Buddha need not necessarily have been taught by the Buddha in his lifetime as a human on this earth.

Individual practitioners, due to the power of the karmic maturation, could have visionary experience of mandala deities and so on, even after the Buddha's death. Based on such mystical encounters, scriptures could come into being. To this day, there are great revealers of "treasure texts" *(terma)*. These masters, with the right qualifications, can reveal texts that have been hidden in the past. Of course, we must consistently watch out for charlatans! But what this possibility reflects is that we do not necessarily need to trace the origin of a Buddhist practice directly to the historical Buddha.

However, there is the problem argued by contemporary scholars that the styles of the composition of many Mahayana scriptures, such as the perfection of wisdom sutras, are relatively recent—that is, those styles were not in vogue at the time of the Buddha. Therefore, they argue that these scriptures cannot be accepted as authentic. An example of this would be the *Kalachakra Tantra*.[13] I concede that the language and the style of composition may not reflect the originality of the Buddha's words, but it is conceivable that the differences in the style of composition result from the differences of the compilers. For example, in Tibetan Buddhism there are many revealed texts attributed to Padmasambhava. Given the different scholastic backgrounds and temperaments of the revealers of these texts, we find diversity in the compositional style even of those texts attributed to Padmasambhava. As this is the case, then the Mahayana scriptures, which are attributed to the Buddha, could easily display a diversity in the style of composition and language due to the different individuals whose visionary, mystical experiences are the basis upon which these scriptural texts were compiled.

Personal Investigation

My defenses of the validity of the Mahayana scriptures may sound a bit haphazard to you. The most convincing method of investigation to determine validity may be to use the scientific method—you should undertake your own investigation. Regardless of whether these scriptures can be proven to be the Buddha's original words, what is important is to determine whether or not they are beneficial. Even if something is the original word of the Buddha, if it is not beneficial—that is, if it does not have any positive effect on you—then there is no value in it. On the other hand, even if it cannot be proven that something is the original word of the Buddha, but it is nevertheless beneficial and effective, then of course it still has great value.

Putting aside Indian history and looking only at the lives of past Tibetan masters, while we have to admit that there may be some exaggerations in the biographies of these lamas, we cannot totally dismiss all of these works as pure fantasy. What seems true is that many great masters attained high realizations. So it is important that we do not entirely get lost in these speculations but rather concentrate more on our own personal spiritual practice. With this kind of approach, we can certainly deepen our conviction in the validity of the Buddha's teachings. I think this is more important than delving into speculative questions as to whether these teachings were historically taught by the Buddha. Having said this, these "proofs" of Mahayana scriptures as being authentic are important. For once suspicions of their validity have been raised, it is normal that we would want some answers that would give us confidence. In this sense, the arguments in these verses are quite valuable.

MEDITATION

Let us now meditate on the theme of the mind. Since all of samsara and nirvana come about from a state of mind—an undisciplined state in the first case and a disciplined state of mind in the second case—the mind is like a creator. Mind is therefore of primary importance. In this meditation session we will examine exactly what this mind is. We will try to identify it.

Generally, when we perceive external objects, because of our habitual attraction to them, they feel familiar. Because of this familiarity, the mind takes on the aspect of that object. For example, when we perceive a vase, sense data similar to the vase arises in our eye sense faculty; the perception arises as if taking on the aspect of that vase. We feel like these perceptions have a kind of tangibility. Since our mind feels somehow fused with that object, the nature of the mind itself remains obscured. This is partly due to our overemphasis on the external world—our objectification of it—and partly because our thoughts are constantly preoccupied with fears and hopes about the future and recollection of the past. We are often caught up in thoughts of regret and desire. All of these factors mean that our present awareness is typically obscured.

What you should do, then, is consciously restrain your mind from recollecting the past or anticipating, fearing, or hoping about the future. Simply focus on the present moment and do not allow your mind to chase after external objects or events. Do not objectify things, but rather remain in the natural state of mind, simply resting in the present moment. In that way, you will be able to experience a certain mental clarity.

This is a bit like water—when there is turbulence, such as waves or bubbles, we cannot see the clarity of the water itself. Once the water stills, we can perceive it clearly, seeing what is in it. Similarly, we should allow our mind to rest and try to free it of turbulent thought bubbles and waves, try to remain in that nonconceptual state.

This, I should mention, is not an especially profound meditative technique. It is found also in non-Buddhist meditative traditions.

So, in this session, try to meditate on this openness or clarity. Stay in this present, empty state of mind, simply being aware of the mind's present moment. Just remain in this nonconceptual state.

7. EMPTINESS ACCORDING TO THE MIDDLE WAY SCHOOL

COMMENTARY

The Minds of Arhats

According to Khenpo Künpal's commentary, Shantideva is here presenting arguments to demonstrate the superiority of the Mahayana path.

> 44. The true monk is the very root of Dharma,
> But difficult it is to be a monk indeed.
> And hard it is for minds enmeshed in thoughts
> To pass beyond the bonds of suffering.
>
> 45. You say there's liberation in the instant
> That defilements are entirely forsaken.
> Yet those who from defilements are set free
> Continue to display the influence of karma.

The text states that if we insist without accepting the doctrine of emptiness that the root of the doctrine is the monastic community, it is impossible for members of the monastic community to become arhats. That is, if the community of arhats is the root of the doctrine, then the very existence of such a community would be implausible if we do not accept the doctrine of emptiness.

To this, Hinayanists might respond that we can posit a community of arhats without accepting the doctrine of emptiness because even without realizing emptiness, it is still possible to attain full liberation from cyclic existence through the realization of the four noble truths. In reply, the Madhyamika states that even in order to gain freedom from cyclic existence, the realization of emptiness is indispensable. For the root cause of bondage to cyclic existence is ignorance grasping at the true existence of phenomena. Without cutting this root cause, there is no possibility of attaining liberation. Without the realization of emptiness, meditating on emptiness will be merely remaining in a nonconceptual state. Simply shutting out thoughts can never lead to full liberation from cyclic existence.

With regard to verse 46, there is a divergence of interpretation between the two Tibetan commentaries. The verse reads:

> 46. "Only for a while," you say. "For it is certain
> That the cause of rebirth, craving, is exhausted."
> They have no craving, granted, through defiled
> motion.
> But how could they avoid the craving linked
> with ignorance?

The Hinayanists respond to Shantideva by arguing that, although these arhats, who have gained liberation from samsara, might not have gained full freedom from the habitual patterns formed by deluded states of mind, on account of having gained liberation they have nonetheless cut the root of cyclic existence, and therefore there is no rebirth for them.

Shantideva states here that only by engaging in a path that involves full realization of both the selflessness of persons and the selflessness of phenomena can we arrive at the state of the

Buddha's full omniscience. According to Shantideva, such a path can be found only in the Mahayana teachings. In this sense, Mahayana scriptures can be seen as being superior to the Hinayana teachings, because it is only in the Mahayana that the path to full enlightenment is found. As for the arhats, who have gained liberation from samsara, Shantideva argues that we can still observe the effects of karmic imprints. For example, in the case of Shariputra and Maudgalyayana, although they have attained liberation from samsara, they are not free from the habitual patterns formed by past deluded states of mind.

Shantideva continues:

> 47. This craving is produced by virtue of sensation,
> And sensation, this they surely have.
> Concepts linger still within their minds,
> And it is to these concepts that they cling.

Shantideva is saying that although these so-called arhats whom the Hinayanist considers fully liberated from samsara may not have craving as such, since they have the fundamental ignorance grasping at a notion of self, a form of attachment can still arise. To this, the Hinayanists could respond that these arhats cannot have any craving because there are no deluded states in the mind. The Madhyamika would then respond to this by stating that because they have sensations, or feelings, these so-called arhats will grasp at these feelings as real, and that will give rise to attachment. Therefore, even from the Hinayanist's point of view, these so-called arhats are not fully liberated from samsara because they still have the potential to take rebirth.

In the next verse Shantideva states that as long as the individual's mind is not freed from the tendency to grasp onto something as real and truly existent, it is not freed from grasping and, therefore, from attachment and craving.

> 48. The mind that has not realized emptiness,
> May be halted, but will once again arise—

Just as from a nonperceptual absorption.
Therefore, emptiness must be cultivated.

As long as craving remains, the conditions for taking rebirth will be present within the individual's mental continuum. Therefore, in a mindstream lacking the realization of emptiness, the factors that bind an individual to cyclic existence will recur.

This is just like the case where someone remains in a nonconceptual, thoughtless state, and when he or she comes out of that absorptive state, the conceptual thought processes start again. Therefore, in order to arrive at the point where we have gained total freedom from all tendencies to cling onto things as truly existing, it is necessary to realize emptiness.

Realization of Emptiness Required Even for Liberation

According to Minyak Künsö's commentary, these verses state that, even to attain liberation from cyclic existence, the realization of emptiness is indispensable. So these verses are related to the main thesis about the indispensability of realizing emptiness. This issue was raised by the Hinayanists when they asked, "What need is there to realize emptiness when by applying the teachings of the four noble truths, we can gain liberation from samsara?" According to this reading, verses 44–48 mean that, if the root of the Buddha's doctrine is the monastic community composed of arhats, then without the doctrine of emptiness, it would be impossible not only to attain the fully enlightened state of buddhahood but also to attain even liberation from samsara. As long as our mind remains fettered by the tendency to objectify, there is no possibility of gaining liberation.

If anyone were to state that we can gain liberation by simply engaging in the path of meditating on the sixteen characteristics of the four noble truths, such as impermanence and so on, and by doing so negate the self as a self-sufficient and substantial reality, the Madhyamika would reject this claim on the ground that this realization of selflessness at such a gross level cannot lead to full liberation. The arhat that the Hinayanists claim to be a fully liberated being is in reality not an arhat, for that person still has, within his or her mental continuum, the tendency to grasp at true and intrinsic existence of phenomena. Such a person would manifest emotions and thoughts, such as craving, and would also display the effects of karmic actions, habitual patterns, and so forth.

The Hinayanists might still maintain that such a person, due to the power of his or her realization of selflessness, is free from craving. The Madhyamika, however, would contend that the Hinayanists' notion of craving remains incomplete—relating only to gross, manifest, and conscious levels of craving. In the mind of an arhat, there are still subtle forms of craving that, by the Hinayanist definition, are not regarded as defilements. However, just as the Hinayanist accepts two types of ignorance—ignorance that is the root cause of cyclic existence and a more subtle ignorance—similarly, we can also posit two types of craving—a more obvious, conscious state of craving and a subtler form. So even within the mind of that so-called arhat, there persists a subtle grasping at true existence. Because of this, there exists in their mental continuum other derivative, deluded states, such as craving and attachment. As long as the tendency remains within any of our psyches for objectifying and grasping at things as truly existent, we cannot be said to be free from craving and attachment.

It is not adequate to realize only the gross levels of selflessness; it is essential to realize the emptiness of intrinsic existence of persons and phenomena as well. As long as we lack this deep insight into the nature of emptiness, although gross levels of negative emotions and thoughts may temporarily subside, since the potential still lies within our psyches, these emotions and afflictive thoughts will recur. Therefore, the realization of emptiness is indispensable not only to attain full enlightenment, but even to attain liberation from cyclic existence.

Prasangika and Svatantrika Understandings of Emptiness

When cultivating the understanding of emptiness, it is critical to recognize that the various Buddhist philosophical schools understand its meaning and scope differently. The Svatantrika-Madhyamikas maintain that all phenomena are devoid of true existence, but what do they mean when they say this? Despite their rejection of true existence, they still hold that all phenomena possess some form of *self-nature (svabhava)* and thus accept a degree of objective existence. That self-nature, or mode of being, they posit in relation to a nondeceptive cognition. In this way they maintain that there is no mode of being that exists autonomously and independently of the perceiving mind. However, because phenomena possess some form of objective reality, valid perceptions are necessarily said to be nondeceptive. The Prasangika-Madhyamaka school, by contrast, attributes no degree of intrinsic nature or objective mode of being to phenomena whatsoever. Even the self-nature accepted by the Svatantrika-Madhyamika becomes an object of negation for the Prasangika-Madhyamika.

For the Prasangika, all our ordinary perceptions are deceptive in some sense. For example, our visual perception of a vase may be valid in relation to the vase, in that it validly perceives the vase, and that its object, the vase, exists. However, that perception is deceptive in that it perceives the vase as existing independently—as if enjoying some kind form of intrinsic reality. In contrast, according to the Svatantrika-Madhyamika, this visual perception of the vase is not only valid in relation to the vase, but also in relation to the intrinsic reality of the vase. The visual perception that apprehends the vase to exist objectively and as possessing self-nature is considered valid. Moreover, the criterion of valid perception, according to the Svatantrika-Madhyamaka school, is that it must be valid with regard to the inherent nature of its perceived object. For the Prasangika-Madhyamika, the vase does not enjoy any objective, intrinsic existence, even in conventional terms, because the Prasangika does not accept the existence of self-nature. Therefore, the visual perception that apprehends its object as objectively existing and enjoying some kind of intrinsic nature is mistaken and deceived.

Thus, although both Madhyamaka schools accept the philosophy of emptiness, the scope of their negations differ. Similarly, although both schools recognize fundamental ignorance as the root cause of all defilements, they differ in their understanding of the subtleties of this misperception. Both accept the fact that our ignorance gives rise to manifest afflictions, such as craving, attachment, and grasping.

Because the Svatantrika-Madhyamikas believe in some kind of intrinsic nature, they do not accept that attraction to objects on the basis of such a belief is deluded. In contrast, the Prasangika-Madhyamikas maintain that such attractions are deluded and are instances of afflictive emotions. So, because there are differences in their identification of the object of negation and their definitions of subtle ignorance, there are differences between the two Madhyamikas in their understanding of the nature of the states of mind that derive from ignorance.

Different Degrees of the Emptiness of Persons

Let us pause and reflect, taking as the object of our analysis the person. We can speak of different degrees of emptiness in relation to persons. For example, we can speak of the person as being absent of any permanent, independent, indivisible reality. Another level of emptiness of the person is the absence of any self-sufficient, self-certifying, and substantial reality. We can also speak of the person as being absent of true existence; and we can speak of the person as being absent of intrinsic existence. So, even in relation to a single phenomenon, such as a person, we can speak of different degrees of subtlety in its emptiness.

The conception of an independent, unitary, and permanent self is the *atman,* or self, posited by non-Buddhist schools in the classical Indian traditions. This self is said to exist independent of the physical and mental aggregates, and such a self is conceived to be the controller or the governor, enjoying a substantial reality. The negation of such a self is one level of the selflessness of persons. Another level of emptiness is the absence or emptiness of the person as the basis or true referent of the term "person." Although the person is the referent of the term "person," it is not so intrinsically—independent of language and thought. The correlation between the person and the term "person" emerges in dependence on convention. Then there is the emptiness of person as truly existent, which is the emptiness of person as defined by the Svatantrika-Madhyamaka school. The subtlest level of emptiness of person is the emptiness of the intrinsic existence of person, which negates any degree of intrinsic personal identity.

So we find five different degrees of selflessness, or emptiness, in relation to one single entity, such as a person. Just as there are different levels of emptiness of persons, there are also five opposite levels of reification. Out of these five, the earlier ones are grosser compared to the later ones. Similarly, we can posit different levels of the derivative afflictions—such as anger, hatred, attachment, jealousy—corresponding to the degrees of reification of persons.

So, what is being stated here in these verses is that the understanding of afflictive emotions and thoughts according to the Hinayana school is relatively coarse and incomplete, and hence a person who has overcome only this level of afflictive emotions and thoughts *cannot* be said to be an arhat, a person who has attained freedom from cyclic existence. Shantideva argues that, according to the Hinayana, a person may have overcome the delusions as defined by the Hinayanist, but as this person has not eliminated the ignorance grasping at the intrinsic existence of phenomena, there still remains within that person's mental continuum derivative afflictive states that will manifest as emotions and thoughts. Therefore, such a person cannot truly have attained liberation from cyclic existence.

Three Extra Verses

The following three verses continue with the comparison of the Mahayana scriptures and the Hinayana scriptures. However, according to the Indian commentator Prajnakaramati, these three verses are not written by Shantideva. In fact, they contribute little to the overall argument.

49. If all that is encompassed by the sutras
You hold to be the Buddha's perfect speech,
Why do you not hold the greater part of Mahayana,
Which with your sutras is in perfect harmony?

50. If, due to just a single jarring element,
The whole is held to be at fault,
How might not a single point in concord with
the sutras
Vindicate the rest as Buddha's teaching?

51. Mahakashyapa himself and others
Could not sound the depths of such a teaching.
Who will therefore say they are to be rejected
Just because they are not grasped by you?

Emptiness Is the Key

There seems to be again a slight difference in the interpretation of the next verse, although I think the two commentaries end up at the same point, which is that a bodhisattva remains free from the two extremes—the extreme of cyclic existence and the extreme of the solitary peace of nirvana.

52. To linger and abide within samsara,
But freed from every craving and from every fear,
To work for the benefit of those who ignorantly suffer:
Such is the fruit that emptiness will bear.

Only by engaging in a path of emptiness does the bodhisattva arrive at buddhahood, which is free from these two extremes. All of the preceding verses are aimed at proving the central thesis—that the realization of emptiness is necessary not just for the attainment of full enlightenment, but also even for attaining liberation from samsara. Bodhisattvas remain within cyclic existence and do not seek the solitary peace of nirvana for their own benefit. Bodhisattvas voluntarily seek to take rebirth in cyclic existence; such is their altruism, which is actually said to be the fruit of meditation on emptiness.

Shantideva then goes on to say that since no valid refutation of emptiness can be found, there is no doubt that realization of emptiness must be cultivated.

53. From this, the emptiness doctrine will be seen
To be immune from all attack.
And so, with every doubt abandoned,
Let us meditate upon this emptiness.

54. Afflictive passion and the veils of ignorance—
The cure for these is emptiness.
Therefore, how could they not meditate upon it
Who wish swiftly to obtain omniscience?

55. Whatever is the source of pain and suffering,
Let that be the object of our fear.
But emptiness will allay our every sorrow;
How could it be for us a thing of dread?

56. If such a thing as "I" exists indeed,
Then terrors, granted, will torment it.
But since no self or "I" exists at all,
What is there left for fears to terrify?

He is stating that the realization of emptiness is in fact the cure for the afflictive emotions and for all the obscurations to knowledge. Therefore, those who seek the attainment of the fully enlightened state of buddhahood and omniscience must swiftly cultivate the understanding of emptiness.

He further states that normally fear arises appropriately toward something that produces suffering, but in the mind of the person who has realized emptiness, there is no room for suffering to arise, for there is simply no basis for it.

Shantideva says that, if there were such a thing called "I" or "self," then there would a basis from which fear could arise. However, since there is no such self, where can fear arise when there is no one to experience that fear? The point he is making is this: If there were some real entity behind the term "I," then there could be fear due to this real "I," but as there is no such thing as the self, then whose fear can it be?

Identitylessness of Persons

Another major section begins with verse 57, presenting detailed reasoning to establish emptiness. The first subdivision of this section is about establishing the identitylessness of persons. As I've already mentioned, emptiness consists of two classes: the emptiness, or identitylessness, of persons and the emptiness of phenomena. In terms of their natures, there is not even a subtle difference between these two classes of emptiness. However, due to the difference of the object upon which the emptiness is established, it is said that the emptiness of persons is easier to realize than that of phenomena. This is reflected in the sequence in which these two emptinesses are presented in the scriptures. Shantideva's text, for example, presents the emptiness of persons first followed by the emptiness of phenomena.

We should understand that intrinsic existence is not like a physical illness or like mental obscurations, which can be removed through a process of awakening. Intrinsic existence is not something that existed in the past that, through practice and meditation, can be removed. It never existed to begin with, whereas the mental obscurations do exist. Thus, negating intrinsic existence is different from eliminating the mental obscurations. The question will arise, "If intrinsic existence was never there from the start, why then do we need to negate it?" Although it has never been there, due to our fundamental ignorance, we experience it as if it really is.

Identifying the Self to Be Negated

So, what is important, as we prepare to understand this section on the emptiness of the self, is to first develop a good understanding of precisely what is to be negated. Meditation on emptiness depends on properly identifying the object of negation. When we speak of emptiness, we should understand that, when things are said to be empty of intrinsic existence, it is not like negating the presence of persons inside a temple. In this example, the basis of emptiness, the temple, and what it is empty of, the people, are two separate entities. However, in the context of negating intrinsic existence, what is being negated is an apparent mode of being of the very object itself.

What is meant by *self* or *identity* when we speak of selflessness or identitylessness? In his commentary on Aryadeva's *Four Hundred Verses,* Chandrakirti states that, within the context of selflessness, *self* means an independent, autonomous being. Whatever things or events we take as an example, if we attribute to them a way of being that is independent, autonomous, and possessing an intrinsic reality, then that perceived characteristic becomes the self that is the object of negation. This mode of being is what we negate within the context of the teachings on selflessness.

This definition of *self* by Chandrakirti is found in his commentary on a particular verse in *Four Hundred Verses,* where he states that no things or events exist by means of autonomous forces. Rather, they exist only by their dependence upon other causes and conditions—other factors. Therefore, they do not possess any ontological status that is independent and autonomous. Such a status is called *self.* Since all things and events are devoid of such independent, autonomous existence, they are said to be absent or empty of *self*-existence.

The sense of self or the thought "I am" that arises in us has different aspects. In his *Supplement to the Middle Way,* Chandrakirti speaks of two aspects of our sense of self: the mere focus of our "I" consciousness, and the object we grasp at as intrinsically existent. The latter is our object of negation, not the former. Chandrakirti states that our sense of self focuses on the conventional "I" that is the subject of all our action and experience. Then, focused on that self, we apprehend it as intrinsically real. This grasping at the intrinsic reality of the self leads us into all sorts of confusion and afflictions, and it is this grasping,

Chandrakirti says, that a yogi must recognize and endeavor to eliminate.

Using philosophical terms, we could make distinctions between, say, an *appearing object* on the one hand and a *referent object of apprehension* on the other. Through simple introspection, however, if we just look at our ordinary feeling of self, of "me," we can detect within that feeling a strong grasping at self, a belief in some intrinsically existing entity. Within our own sense of personal identity, this belief in an autonomous, unitary agent is strong and instinctive. Changkya Rolpai Dorje writes that some of his contemporaries seemed to believe in an independently existing self "out there" that is the object of negation, while leaving their own innate apprehensions of selfhood intact. However, there is no object of negation separate from the self that is the object of our innate grasping. The very appearance of self to our ordinary, commonsense experience contains within it all the objects of negation. If our understanding of emptiness is such that, while engaged in the negation of selfhood, we get caught up in a verbal game, using exotic terms like *true existence* and *intrinsic existence,* then we risk leaving our instinctive grasping at self untouched and intact. We might seek an imagined self that, in actual fact, has no bearing on our instinctive sense of selfhood. If we fall into this trap, we will not succeed in the negation of the self, and we will leave our innate self-grasping unscathed. We will have managed to negate, at best, only a very gross aspect of the object of negation.

The great Tsongkhapa says that one of the most difficult points in Madhyamaka philosophy is maintaining the reality of the world of conventional truth following the negation of the intrinsic existence of all phenomena. As I mentioned earlier, the qualm that quite naturally arises in our mind is this: "Following the negation of the intrinsic existence of phenomena, how can I coherently think and talk about identity?" This question points to the crux of the philosophical problem. It is useful to make distinctions between the *appearing object* and *referent object,* as this helps us be precise in not negating the actual existence of the self.

If there were no self at all, why aspire to enlightenment? Why seek the path of perfection? There would be no point at all, because there would be no one to attain freedom or perfection!

According to Tsongkhapa, except for the direct realization of emptiness, all our perceptions and experiences are tainted by the apprehension of intrinsic existence. We need to be thorough in identifying the object of negation. We need to utilize our own personal experience and examine how the innate sense of self arises instinctively within. We need to question our experience carefully. If the self to be negated were to exist, in what manner would it exist? We should at least have some sense of what this hypothetical self would be like. Only through a careful examination of the way we actually experience the self will we be able to understand how realizing emptiness can negate the apprehension of intrinsic existence.

In his *Four Hundred Verses,* Aryadeva states that the seed of cyclic existence is consciousness, and only by apprehending the selflessness of objects—in this case, consciousness—can we uproot that seed. When we realize the emptiness of intrinsic existence at a deep level, there is definitely a marked decrease in the force of our afflictions, such as anger and attachment, toward the objects of these emotions. It is as if the realization of emptiness loosens the grip of our afflictions.

Among any gathering of people, each person has his or her own individual fears, hopes, and problems; we see a multiplicity of mental states. Each of these diverse states lacks grounding, or a solid foundation, no matter how forcefully they are felt. Devoid of intrinsic reality, they yet appear as if they do have a firm grounding. It is almost like a magic show conjured by a highly skilled magician. The nature of that reality is, in the final analysis, unfindable. Does it sound strange?

In our daily lives we work hard, often motivated by intense emotional states such as anger, pride, and attachment. What exactly are the objects toward which our intense emotions are directed? If we were to search for them, would we find them? Is there anything actually to be found? This is the way we need to question our everyday experience. If, however, as a result of your critical thinking, you conclude that there is no point even in seeking buddhahood because it is devoid of intrinsic existence, this is an indication that you are beginning to slide into nihilism.

Dromtönpa once said that within the sphere of emptiness, a hand is empty and fire is empty, but if you put your hand into the fire, the fire will burn you! I think this is very true. If you go to people who say, "Oh, everything is like an illusion, everything is like a dream, nothing is real," and prick them with a needle, how do they react? Let them find out if there is a reality! I am not stating that things do not exist—things and events do exist, they do impact our experiences of pain and pleasure. What is being stated here is that things do not exist the way we perceive them to exist.

The Unfindability of the Self

Within our apprehension of true existence, there are two types. First is the innate or instinctual, which can be found even in the mindstreams of animals, and second is the apprehension of selfhood that comes about through the process of reasoning or philosophical thinking. This second type of apprehension is known as *intellectually acquired grasping at selfhood.* The root of cyclic existence is the first—the innate grasping at intrinsic existence. As an aid or a step toward uprooting this innate, instinctual grasping, we can first dispel the intellectually acquired grasping at the intrinsic existence of phenomena.

As I've stated, it is obvious that the self or person that interacts with others and the world, and that experiences pain and pleasure, exists. However, at the root of our instinctive experience of self, there is an underlying belief in a self that is unitary, autonomous, and enjoys some kind of intrinsic reality. If such a self truly exists, then when we search for it, we should be able to find it. The more we search for the reality of such a self, the clearer and clearer it should become. It is true that the self does not exist *independently* of the composite of body and mind, but it also does not exist as it appears to our instinctual, innate sense of self. If an intrinsically real self exists, then it should exist within the physical and mental aggregates that constitute a person. In other words, it should be findable within our body and mind.

Nagarjuna states in his *Precious Garland (Ratnavali)* that the person is not the earth element, nor the fire, water, air, or space element. Neither does the person exist independently of these elements.[14] So, if we were to search for the person or the self, we would be unable to locate it within the constituents of the body. Likewise, if we try to locate the self within the continuum of consciousness, we will fail to find it there as well. The consciousness is the consciousness *of* a person; it cannot *be* the person. Similarly, the person is not the composite of body and consciousness or the continuum of the composite. If we were to search for the true referent behind the term *person* or *self,* we could not find it individually among the various parts of the body nor within any instant of the consciousness. We could find it neither together with nor separate from the composite of body and mind. In short, there is nothing whatsoever to be found within the continuum of the consciousness and body that can be identified as the true referent of *person* or *self.*

Nagarjuna states in his *Stanzas on the Fundamental Wisdom of the Middle Way (Mulamadhyamakakarika)* that even the Tathagata—the Buddha, toward whom we cultivate faith and devotion—cannot be found if we search for the true referent of the term *Tathagata*.[15] The Buddha's aggregates, his body and mind, cannot be posited as the Buddha; neither can the Buddha be identified independently of his body and mind. The Buddha does not inherently possess the aggregates; nor are the aggregates inherently the basis of the Buddha. When we search through such an analysis, even the Buddha turns out to be unfindable. What exactly do we mean when we say that things and events are empty? Since all things and events come into being as the aggregation of causes and conditions—other factors beside themselves—they are therefore devoid of any self-sufficient, independent nature. That absence of any independent nature or intrinsic reality is emptiness. It is a mistake to think of emptiness as some ontological category separate from the things and events.

So, in returning to Shantideva's text, we find his next concern is to set out a series of contemplations that analyze the various parts of the body, questioning whether each element of the body is the person.

57. The teeth, the hair, the nails are not the "I,"
And "I" is not the bones or blood;
The mucus from the nose, and phlegm, are not the "I,"
And neither is it made of lymph or pus.

58. The "I" is not the body's grease or sweat,
The lungs and liver likewise do not constitute it.
Neither are the inner organs "I,"
Nor yet the body's excrement and waste.

59. The flesh and skin are not the "I,"
And neither are the body's warmth and breath.
The cavities within the frame are not the "I,"
And "I" is not accounted for within the six perceptions.

And we will see below that Shantideva continues with a series of contemplations on the various aspects of consciousnesses and other factors of existence, enquiring further whether any of these can be posited as the real person.

MEDITATION

Now try to meditate on emptiness. As Shantideva states in this text, it is quite evident that if we search for the "self," it is unfindable. However, the implication of this is not that the self does not exist, for we know from our personal experience that we undergo pain and pleasure. We know that it is something or someone who has these experiences. However, if we search for it, it is unfindable. The conclusion we arrive at, therefore, is that the self can only be said to exist nominally, by the power of conceptual designation.

With this thought in the background, try and examine how things, including your own self, appear to your mind. Do they appear as if they possess only nominal status, or do they appear to you in a different light? Certainly they do not appear as being only nominally real; they appear to possess some kind of objective, intrinsic existence—to exist in their own right. They do not appear to exist by the power of designation; they appear to enjoy an objective, independent status. What we arrive at, then, as a result of our reflection, is a deep conviction that things do not exist in the manner in which they appear.

While resting in meditative equipoise on emptiness, you should not have even lingering feelings that "This is emptiness" or "I am meditating on emptiness." You should instead try to remain absorbed single-pointedly in the mere absence of intrinsic existence—the unfindability of phenomena when searched for through critical enquiry. It should be as if your mind has become fused with emptiness. You should not have any sense of a subject-and-object duality, as if you are observing something "out there." Like this, meditate now for a few minutes on emptiness.

8. THE NATURE AND EXISTENCE OF SELF

PRACTICING WISDOM

Compassion Is Built on Realizing Emptiness

Nagarjuna states that *bodhichitta,* the altruistic mind of awakening, is the root of enlightenment and that it should be complemented by the wisdom that realizes emptiness. So, if we aspire to attain full enlightenment, we must actualize within ourselves this root, the basis of that attainment. And the root of this altruistic mind of awakening is *great compassion,* whose complementary and enhancing factor is the wisdom realizing emptiness.[16] These three factors—bodhichitta, great compassion, and the wisdom of emptiness—constitute the essence of the path to full enlightenment. With the practice of these three elements of the path, we can attain the fully omniscient state; when they are absent, buddhahood is impossible. We could say that these three aspects of the path are the necessary and sufficient conditions for attaining buddhahood.

We have been discussing the view of emptiness and how the wisdom that realizes emptiness has the capacity to eradicate our fundamental ignorance and thereby lead us to freedom from suffering. It is through the realization of emptiness that we are able to recognize that the ignorant mind that grasps at the intrinsic existence of phenomena is distorted. Because it is a state of mind, it can be removed. So, the potential for liberation exists naturally within all beings. Once we have realized the emptiness of intrinsic existence, it is also possible to develop a genuine sense of powerful compassion toward all sentient beings, who are caught in cyclic existence due to their fundamental ignorance of the nature of reality.

The Power of Compassion

Of course, for practicing Buddhists, compassion is crucial to their spiritual path. Generally, too, we can say that the more altruistic and compassionate a person is, the more the person will be committed to the well-being of other sentient beings. Even from the point of view of personal self-interest, the stronger the force of someone's compassion, the more courageous and determined that person will be. All major world religions agree on the importance of compassion. It is not just highly praised: great attention is given to the promotion of compassion as well. There exists in the teachings of these great religions various practical methods for developing compassion. Of course there are differences in philosophy and metaphysics, and, given this diversity, there are also slight differences in how compassion is defined—the understanding of its scope and so on. All the great traditions converge, however, on stressing that compassion is critically important and that its practice has to do with developing our natural capacity for empathy, sharing in the suffering of others.

It seems that when we have a compassionate heart, we also have greater courage and determination. Why is this so? I think it is because when we have compassion in our heart, we are not absorbed in our own stresses and conflicts. Rather, we tend to pay greater attention to the suffering and well-being of other beings, and we are better able to relate to others' suffering based on our own experience. As a result, our perspective, and in some cases even the actual experience of our own suffering, pain, and problems, change. What may seem unbearable can appear less significant—even minor. So to someone who is altruistic and compassionate, there will be a sense that his or her own problems and conflicts become quite tolerable. These adversities then have less potential to disturb our peace of mind.

The compassionate state of mind that is infused with a sense of deep concern for the well-being of other sentient beings is arrived at through reasoned consideration, through systematically cultivated thought processes. This powerful sentiment may be accompanied by other forceful emotions, yet when such emotions arise, there will hardly be any room for these to disturb our mind. This is because these emotions are grounded in reasoned considerations—that is, the faculty of human intelligence plays a great role in their development. In contrast, in our day-to-day life, we often encounter situations and experiences that provoke us into emotional explosions. I consider these types of responses to trivial incidents as afflictive, because they only cause disturbance and throw our mind off balance. If our mindstream is infused with compassionate thoughts and a good heart, adversities that would normally give rise to a strong emotional reaction do not provoke us. There is an underlying stability and rootedness.

Sharing in the Pain of Others

Often people think of compassion as a feeling of pity, and regard the person who is the object of compassion as somewhat inferior. I do not think this is correct. Genuine compassion must arise from recognizing that other beings—just like ourselves—desire happiness and wish to overcome suffering. Based on this, a genuine empathy or connectedness arises when we encounter others' suffering. This is genuine compassion. We feel responsible toward the other and a deep concern for the other's welfare. There is therefore an underlying recognition of utter equality between ourselves and others. There is a genuine respect for others' natural aspiration to attain happiness and to overcome suffering, and a recognition of their right to fulfill that aspiration.

When compassion is generated, because of our deep contemplation of others' suffering and sharing in it, it is possible that this could disturb our mental calm to some extent. Therefore, we may want to ask, "When cultivating compassion, are we not taking upon ourselves additional suffering?" I think this is a critical question and requires serious thought.

To begin with, I feel there is a big difference between the pain and suffering that we undergo naturally as part of our own cycle of life and what we experience as a result of voluntarily sharing in others' suffering. In our own case, we undergo pain and suffering with no real say in the matter. We have no control over what we experience. In the case of others, the equilibrium in our mind may be slightly disturbed, but because we have taken it upon ourselves voluntarily for a specific purpose, the effect on our mind is totally different. I don't think we get totally overwhelmed by the suffering and pain. Instead of an agonizing burden, I think that deep down there is a sense of joy, of confidence borne of strength.

To develop such a powerful state of mind as compassion, which has great spiritual value and benefits, it is not adequate merely to contemplate the suffering of others. It is important to first reflect upon your own suffering and develop a deep sense of its unbearableness. As this feeling deepens and becomes stronger, you will be better able to empathize with others' suffering. Generally, when we see beings who are in acute pain, we naturally feel compassionate. However, if we see someone who is, in our eyes, successful in worldly terms—wealthy, powerful, and with lots of friends—instead of feeling compassion toward such a person, we may feel envy. This shows that our realization of the suffering nature of human existence is not profound. It is crucial to first generate a deep insight into the suffering nature of our own existence.

A Step-by-Step Approach

We should not only recognize evident sufferings as painful and undesirable, we must also recognize as undesirable the suffering of change and, most importantly, the pervasive suffering of conditioning. The point here is that we need to engage in a path with a step-by-step approach. We need, therefore, a combined approach of analytic meditation on the one hand and absorptive meditation on the other. Since compassion is a quality of the mind, and since the mind has a never-ending continuum, if you pursue this path of combining meditation of analysis and absorption for a long time, your spiritual practice will acquire a stable basis.

This stable basis becomes part of the mind through the force of habit. Those who believe in rebirth will look at two children of the same family and speak of their having different predispositions carried over from the past. We say that this child has one kind of predisposition, while the other is inclined differently. Although the body is new to this lifetime, the consciousness continues from the previous life. It is in this sense that the qualities in the mindstream are believed to be stable and enduring.

In contrast, people have other qualities, such as athletic prowess, that are entirely contingent upon the body. There is a limit to how much we can enhance this capacity—it is not limitless. For example, regardless of how talented an athlete may be, he or she can only jump so much. Furthermore, these qualities endure only as long as the physical conditions remain intact. They cannot be carried over into the next life. The continuum of the mind, however, does carry on. Therefore, a quality based on the mind is more enduring.

So, through training the mind, qualities such as compassion, love, and the wisdom realizing emptiness can be developed. Through familiarization these qualities can be developed to their highest potentials. Although initially it may require a good deal of effort, once you get beyond a certain point, the development becomes spontaneous, natural, and self-sustaining. There is no need for further effort. This is why we can say that these qualities can be developed infinitely.

If we interrupt our athletic training, we will have to go through the whole training procedure again to bring our skill back to its previous level. However, once we have developed a quality of the mind to a level of spontaneity, although we may leave it aside for a long time, a slight application will bring it back to the prior level. The difference between the two qualities is due to the difference of their bases, mental and physical.

In this way, the development of the mind through successive lifetimes is understood. Even if you do not make much headway in this lifetime, because the qualities acquired in the mind will be retained, these predispositions can be activated in the future.

In order to enhance our potential for compassion to its infinite level, the realization of emptiness is indispensable. From our personal experience we can see that when our mind remains in a state of confusion, uncertainty, and ignorance, then even short moments of time can be painful and agonizing. On the other hand, if our mind is filled with wisdom and insight, although a task may involve great emotional hardship, we do not feel that this is an ordeal. Therefore, it is important to enhance our wisdom by cultivating an understanding of emptiness. For that, it is necessary to study texts outlining the doctrine of emptiness, such as Shantideva's *The Way of the Bodhisattva*.

COMMENTARY

Refuting Non-Buddhist Views of Self

We continue the discussion of the emptiness, or identitylessness, of persons now with Shantideva's refutation of the self posited by various philosophical schools, particularly the Samkhya school, which identifies the self as an independent, autonomous consciousness. The other school whose views are negated here is the Vaisheshika, which accepts a notion of self as a material, autonomous, and independent reality. These two views of self are negated in verses 60–69.

I will not go into great detail about the refutation of self as posited by these non-Buddhist schools, but some context is necessary. The essence of the Samkhya's theory of self is a classification of reality into twenty-five categories, twenty-three of which are manifestations of one called the primal substance. The remaining category is the self, which is conceived as a cognitive awareness that is an autonomous reality. The twenty-three categories are thought of as "enjoyments" of the self. The Samkhyas maintain that as long as we remain unenlightened, we are ignorant of the fact that all these categories are created by the primal substance, and we therefore remain in a world of multiplicity and duality. However, they say, when we realize that these categories are actually manifestations of the primal substance, then the self becomes liberated and the world of duality and appearances dissolves. The specific refutation of the Samkhyas' concept of primal substance, which they define as the state of equilibrium of three forces—the neutral, positive, and negative forces—comes later in the text. At this point, only their conception of self is being refuted by Shantideva.

According to Samkhya, the self "enjoys" because it is the subject that experiences pain and pleasure, and so on. It is permanent because it is not born and does not die. It is devoid of any functions, for it is not the creator of all the manifestations at the level of multiplicity. Because the self does not possess the qualities of the three fundamental aspects—neutral, positive, and negative—it is free of these characteristics. These characteristics of the self are in contrast with the primal substance. Since the self is all-pervasive, it has no specific functions as such. In its nature, the self is consciousness. Because it is indivisible, it is a unitary reality—infinite, limitless, and all-pervasive. These are the characteristics of self as conceived by the Samkhya. In the following verses, Shantideva draws our attention to the contradictions involved in this conception of the self. Of course, if you actually come across a learned, non-Buddhist Indian scholar, he may well have many arguments in defense of this view!

The verses begin by supposing that, if the consciousness of sound is the permanent self, then how can the Samkhya state that it has a function of cognition?

60. If the hearing consciousness is permanent,
It follows that it's hearing all the time.
If there is no object, what is knowing what?
Why do you now say that there is consciousness?

61. If consciousness is that which does not know,
It follows that a stick is also conscious.
Therefore, in the absence of a thing to know,
It is clear that consciousness will not arise.

How can you attribute to the self the quality of knowing? You would be implying that if the self is the consciousness of sound, then sound will be perceived at all times. On the other hand, if you assert that cognitions exist even in the absence of their objects—such as sound—then it follows that a piece of wood could be conscious, since cognitions do not require objects. You have to agree then, that without objects of cognition, there can be no cognitions. Shantideva continues:

62. "But consciousness may turn to apprehend
a form," you say.
But why, then, does it cease to hear?
Perhaps you say the sound's no longer there.
If so, the hearing consciousness is likewise absent.

63. How could that which has the nature of
perceiving sound
Be changed into a form-perceiver?
"A single man," you say, "can be both son and father."
But these are merely names; his nature is not so.

64. Thus "pleasure," "pain," "neutrality"
Do not partake of fatherhood or sonship,
And we indeed have never yet observed
A consciousness of form perceiving sound.

65. "But like an actor," you will say, "it takes on
 different roles."
 If so, this consciousness is not a changeless thing.
 "It's one thing," you will say, "with different modes."
 That's unity indeed, and never seen before!

66. "But different modes," you claim, "without reality."
 And so its essence you must now describe.
 You say that this is simply knowing—
 All beings therefore are a single thing.

67. What has mind and what does not have mind
 Are likewise one, for both are equal in existing.
 If the different features are deceptive,
 What is the support that underlies them?

Next follows the refutation of the Vaisheshika theory of self. In this view, self is posited as being an inanimate, material substance.

68. Something destitute of mind, we hold, cannot be self,
 For mindlessness means matter, like a vase.
 "But," you say, "the self has consciousness,
 when joined to mind."
 But this refutes its nature of unconsciousness.

69. If the self, moreover, is immutable,
 What change in it could mingling with the
 mind produce?
 And selfhood we might equally affirm
 Of empty space, inert and destitute of mind.

The Continuity of the Conventional Self

The following short section, verses 70–77, are Shantideva's answers to the objections against the emptiness of self. One objection is that if the self does not exist, then the law of karma will become inoperable. This is a criticism of the Madhyamaka rejection of the self as conceived by other schools.

70. "If," you ask, "the self does not exist,
How can acts be linked with their results?
If when the deed is done, the doer is no more,
Who is there to reap the karmic fruit?"

The key point being raised is that if we do not accept an enduring, permanent self that comes from the previous life to this life and carries on its continuum in the future, then—even within one single lifetime—we have no connection between the person who accumulates the karma and the one who experiences its effect. Without a self, they object, how can we maintain these two people as the same person? If they are not identical, this contradicts fundamental principles of the karmic law.

According to the principles of karma, no one can experience consequences of karmic acts they did not commit. Conversely, individuals must inevitably face the karmic consequences of their actions unless the potencies of the karmic deeds are somehow neutralized. Therefore, if the person who accumulates karma and the person who experiences the fruition are two separate people, the law of karma is violated.

Shantideva's response to this objection is found in the next verse.

71. The basis of the act and fruit are not the same,
And thus a self lacks scope for its activity.
On this, both you and we are in accord—
What point is there in our debating?

72. A cause coterminous with its result
Is something quite impossible to see.
And only in the context of a single mental stream
Can it be said that one who acts will later reap the fruit.

In other words, the karmic action is the cause, and the fruition of this is its consequence. However, from the point of view of time, the identity of the person who was responsible for the karmic act in the past and that of the person who undergoes the consequences are not one and the same. One exists at a particular time, while the other exists at another time.

To maintain their identity as one and the same in time would contradict even our ordinary conventions and experience. Their relationship as the same person is maintained because they share a single continuum of existence. Although the person undergoes moment-by-moment change, the basic continuum remains.

We can take the example of the continuum of our own body. From a physiological perspective, all our cells are completely different now than when we were younger. At the cellular level, there has been a total change. In fact, this change allows us to speak about a process of aging. What is so beautiful and attractive at a young age later becomes wrinkled and unattractive. However, in terms of the continuum, it is the same body. Because of this, we can make such statements as, "I read such-and-such a book when I was young."

If we assume an identity of the same individual through time, on the basis of the mental continuum, then we can trace the continuity even further. For example, if as a result of heightened awareness, we are able to recall past lives, then we can say that when I was such-and-such, I was born here, and we can speak about a continuum of a single person through a much longer time frame. It is on the basis of this continuum of the consciousness that we can speak of the relationship between karma and its fruition.

For the Madhyamika, such as Shantideva, there is no intrinsically existing self; the self is thought of as a nominal convention. From this point of view we can speak of different aspects of the self. For example, we can speak of the self that came from a previous life that is the same as the self in this particular life. We can speak of a particular person as, say, a Tibetan self, qualified by an ethnic identity, or we can speak of the self of a fully ordained monk, and so on. Thus, even on the basis of one individual, we can speak of different aspects of the self. In the case of a particular individual, we can say that he is a man, a Tibetan person, a Buddhist, a monk, or a fully ordained monk, and so forth. Although all of these different aspects of the self belong to one and the same individual, they did not all come into being simultaneously. The identity of these evolved in different contexts and circumstances.

So, from the point of view of the continuum, we can maintain that the self is, in some sense, permanent or eternal without contradicting that the self is momentarily changing. From the point of view of its moment-by-moment change, the self is transient and impermanent. Thus, there is no contradiction in maintaining that in terms of its continuum, it is eternal, yet in terms of its momentary existence, it is impermanent. Of course, I am not suggesting that the self is permanent in the sense of unchanging!

Is the Mind the Self?

Since Madhyamikas accept a self nominally designated on the basis of body and mind, can the self can be identified with the mind? Among the various Buddhist philosophical schools, a few do maintain, in the final analysis, that the consciousness is the self. For example, the Indian master Bhavaviveka states in his *Blaze of Reasoning* that, effectively, the continuum of the mental consciousness (the sixth consciousness) is the self. Prasangika-Madhyamikas do not accept this view. From their point of view, nothing whatsoever among the bases of designation—neither the bodily continuum nor the consciousness—can be regarded as the self, or the person.

Shantideva, for instance, asks that if we are to posit consciousness as the self, then which one do we choose?

> 73. The thoughts now passed, and those to come,
> are not the self;
> They are no more, or are not yet.
> Is then the self the thought which now is born?
> If so, it sinks to nothing when the latter fades.

Is it the past consciousness, or that which will come in the future, or is it the present? The past consciousness has already ceased, and the future is yet to come. If the present moment of consciousness is the self, then, since it is momentary, once it ceases to exist, the self or person would also cease to exist. Also, if consciousness is the self, then the concept of subject and object becomes untenable. Also, the self and its consciousness cannot be said to have any relationship since, in the final analysis, consciousness *is* the person.

Preserving the Relative World

Shantideva next states, briefly, that as in the case of a banana tree, no matter how much peeling we do, we cannot find any core.

> 74. For instance, we may take banana trees—
> Cutting through the fibers, finding nothing.
> Likewise, analytical investigation
> Will find no "I," no underlying self.

Similarly, when we search for the self among the aggregates—body, feeling, perceptions, consciousness—what we find is only the unfindability of the self. No real core to our being can be identified as the real self.

The next objection raised against the Madhyamika's rejection of self asks: if self does not exist, then there are no sentient beings; if there are no sentient beings, then toward whom do we generate compassion?

> 75. "If beings," you will say, "have no existence,
> Who will be the object of compassion?"
> Those whom ignorance imputes and vows to save,
> Intending thus to gain the lofty goal.

Shantideva responds to this by saying that although there is no independently existing self and therefore no independently existing sentient beings, within the framework of the relative truth, there are sentient beings. By "ignorance" here, Shantideva is not referring to the grasping at intrinsic existence, the fundamental ignorance that is at the root of our unenlightened existence. What he is saying is similar to the statement found in Chandrakirti's *Supplement to the Middle Way,* where the universe is said to be the product of the ignorant mind. Shantideva says that within the framework of relative truth—that is, within the validity of the conventional world of everyday experience—self does exist. Therefore, sentient beings exist for whom we can generate compassion, and these sentient beings have real suffering.

Shantideva next considers a follow-up objection, asking, if there are no sentient beings, then are there are no practitioners of the path who attain the goal?

> 76. "Since beings are no more," you ask, "who gains the fruit?"
> It's true! The aspiration's made in ignorance.
> But for the total vanquishing of sorrow,
> The goal, which ignorance conceives, should not be spurned.

Shantideva acknowledges that this is very true, but states that if we are not content with the validity of the conventional world and seek what is beyond it, we will not find any sentient beings. Within the framework of the relative world, however, there are sentient beings who suffer. So, to gain freedom from suffering, we can engage in a path that will lead to the elimination of the cause—ignorance. This is the ignorant mind grasping at the intrinsic existence of things and events. In essence, what is being stated here is that it is the causal ignorance—which gives rise to suffering, confusion, and so on—that must be rooted out, and not the reality of the conventional world. The world of relativity, the world of cause and effect, is not to be negated.

The question could now be raised: if the reality of the conventional world is not to be negated, then don't we conventionally accept that things and events possess some form of objective, independent status—that something can be pointed out as the true referent of our terms and concepts? Do you also mean that that cannot be destroyed?

77. The source of sorrow is the pride of saying "I,"
Fostered and increased by false belief in self.
To this you may say that there's no redress,
But meditation on no-self will be the supreme way.

Shantideva responds by saying that grasping onto that form of existence is indeed the source of suffering, and gives rise to anger, desire, and delusions. These in turn cause the grasping onto self to increase further, so this ignorant grasping mind needs to be eliminated.

Although we might agree on the need to eliminate this grasping, one could ask whether that is actually possible, and if so, how? Shantideva's response is that we *can* eliminate this ignorance because we can develop its opposing state of mind, the insight into emptiness. This insight directly opposes the way our mind grasps onto a nonexistent self. Since, in reality, there is no such self, the insight that penetrates into the nature of reality perceives its absence. Thus, meditation on emptiness is firmly based on reason and can therefore eliminate the ignorant mind that grasps onto the intrinsic existence of the self.

MEDITATION

Now meditate on compassion. For this, first visualize a sentient being who is going through acute pain or suffering. Focus on that being and develop the thought that just like me, that sentient being possesses the natural aspiration to be happy and overcome suffering. And not only do they wish to overcome suffering, they also have the capacity to do so. Then remind yourself that the root cause of suffering is the misperceiving mind grasping at intrinsic existence, a distorted mind that has the potential to be eliminated. This can be achieved by generating a deep insight into the nature of emptiness. Reflect upon these potentials. We should then develop a deep compassion for all beings and try to enhance that capacity within.

With these thoughts as a background, focus on one sentient being and then gradually extend your contemplation to other sentient beings, such as your neighbors. Then expand it further, seeing if you can also include people you do not like, such as those who have harmed you. Reflect upon their feelings. Regardless of how they behave toward you, reflect that, like you, they too have the natural desire to be happy and to overcome suffering.

Because of the fundamental equality of all beings in having this natural aspiration to be happy and to overcome suffering, we can develop empathy and strong compassion toward each and every being. By training our mind by focusing on specific beings—friends, enemies, and neutral people—we will be able to extend compassion toward everyone. This point is critical. Otherwise, we risk having the idea that there are faceless sentient beings out there toward whom we can develop compassion, but then fail to generate any compassion toward the people with whom we have direct contact, especially our neighbors. This type of discriminatory attitude might arise in us. Try to be aware of this practical concern while meditating on compassion.

9. THE NATURE OF PHENOMENA

COMMENTARY

The Whole and Its Parts

Next follows Shantideva's presentation of the identitylessness, or selflessness, of phenomena, which is explained first by means of the *four mindfulnesses*—mindfulness of the body, of feelings, of mind, and of phenomena. So, according to Shantideva's text, first we reflect upon the nature of our own body. This is done by contemplating the body's general and specific characteristics. These include, for example, the aging process and the impure substances that constitute bodily existence. I won't go into the details of this contemplation here.

Generally speaking, meditating on the mindfulness of body, reflecting upon the nature of our own body, is the approach explained in the Hinayana scriptures. However, we can extend this contemplation to the nature of the body, feelings, mind, and phenomena of all beings, who are limitless like space. Then it becomes a training of the mind according to the Mahayana path. When we contemplate the emptiness of these four factors—body, feelings, mind, and phenomena—we are practicing a mindfulness meditation focused on the ultimate truth.

The Way of the Bodhisattva gives us a systematic practice for these four mindfulness meditations on emptiness. Let us take as our example the human body. It is composed of many different parts—head, arms, legs, and so on. There is also the whole—the body as a complete unit. Generally when we think of *body,* it appears to our mind, at least on the surface, as if there is a single entity that we can point to as a tangible, unitary reality. Based on this commonsense view, we can speak of various characteristics and parts of the body. In other words, we feel as if there is fundamentally a thing called *body,* and we can speak about its parts. Yet if we search for this "body" apart from its various parts, we come to realize that it is actually not to be found.

This is what Shantideva means in the following verses.

78. What we call the body is not feet or shins,
The body, likewise, is not thighs or loins.
It's not the belly nor indeed the back,
And from the chest and arms the body is not formed.

79. The body is not ribs or hands,
Armpits, shoulders, bowels, or entrails;
It is not the head or throat:
From none of these is "body" constituted.

We have a concept of our body as a unitary entity, which we hold to be precious and dear. Yet if we look more carefully, we find that the body is not the feet, nor the calves, the thighs, the hips, the abdomen, the back, the chest, the arms, the hands, the side of the torso, the armpits, the shoulders, the neck, nor the head or any other parts. So where is "body" to be found? If, on the other hand, the body were identical to the individual parts of the body, then the very idea of the body as a unitary entity would be untenable.

80. If "body," step by step,
Pervades and spreads itself throughout its members,
Its parts indeed are present in the parts,
But where does "body," in itself, abide?

81. If "body," single and entire,
Is present in the hand and other members,
However many parts there are, the hand and
all the rest,
You'll find an equal quantity of "bodies."

If this unitary, single entity called *body* is identical to, or exists separately in, each individual part, then just as there are various parts of the body, the body too will become multiple.

Therefore, continues Shantideva, the body does not exist as identical to the individual parts of the body, nor can it exist separately and independently of these parts.

82. If "body" is not outside or within its parts,
How is it, then, residing in its members?
And since it has no basis other than its parts,
How can it be said to be at all?

83. Thus there is no "body" in the limbs,
But from illusion does the idea spring
And is affixed to a specific shape,
Just as when a scarecrow is mistaken for a man.

So how can this body be autonomous, independent, and self-existent? If we carefully examine the nature of the body, we find that the body is nothing more than a designation that we assign on the basis of the aggregation of various parts. We might ask, "What then is the body?" Due to circumstantial conditions such as the lighting, appearance of the object, and so on, we can sometimes mistake a certain shape as a human being.

Similarly, says Shantideva, as long as the appropriate conditions and factors are assembled that give rise to the sense of there being a person, then we can conventionally posit the concept of *body* on that basis.

84. As long as the conditions are assembled,
    A body will appear and seem to be a man.
    As long as all the parts are likewise present,
    It's there that we will see a body.

However, if we search for the true referent behind the term *body,* then we will find nothing. The upshot is that we arrive at the conclusion that "body" is, in the final analysis, a conventional construction—a relative truth—that comes into being only by depending on various causes and conditions.

This above analysis can also be extended to the individual parts of the body, as Shantideva does in the next verses.

85. Likewise, since it is a group of fingers,
    The hand itself is not a single entity.
    And so it is with fingers, made of joints;
    And joints themselves consist of many parts.

86. These parts themselves will break down into atoms,
    And atoms will divide according to direction.
    These fragments, too, will also fall to nothing.
    Thus atoms are like empty space—they have
    no real existence.

When we speak of a hand, we find that it also is a composite of various parts. If a hand existed intrinsically and independently, this would contradict its having the nature of being dependent on other factors. If we search for a hand itself, we do not find a hand separate from the various parts that form it. Just as with a hand, a finger too is a composite that when dissected loses its existence. So with any part of the body, if we search for the true referent behind its name, nothing is to be found.

When we dissect the parts even into their elemental constituents—molecules, atoms, and so on—these too become unfindable. We can carry on dividing even the atoms themselves in terms of their directional surfaces and find, again, that the very idea of *atom* is a mental construct. If we carry on still further, we find that the very idea of matter, or atoms, becomes untenable. In order for anything to be characterized as material, it must have parts. Once we go beyond that and dissect further, what remains is nothing but emptiness.

To our commonsense view, things and events appear as if they have some form of independent and objective status. However, as Shantideva points out in the next verse, if we search for the true nature of such phenomena, we eventually arrive at their unfindability.

> 87. All form, therefore, is like a dream,
> And who will be attached to it, who thus
> investigates?
> The body, in this way, has no existence;
> What is male, therefore, and what is female?

So, we can see that there is nothing absolute about the objects of our anger and attachment. Nothing is desirable or perfect in the absolute sense, neither is anything undesirable and repulsive in the absolute sense. Therefore, in reality, there is no ground for extreme emotional reactions to things and events. Since the body cannot be found when sought through critical analysis, so the designations we make on the basis of the existence of the body—such as differences of gender and race—are also ultimately devoid of essence. So now, what grounds do we have to generate extreme and volatile emotional responses to people of different gender or race?

How Do Things Exist?

When we examine the phenomenological experience of emotions coming and going within us, there is, generally speaking, the appearance that all the things and events each have an independent and objective reality. This is especially so with a strong negative emotion like hatred. We impose a kind of concreteness upon the object such that the object appears to us in sharper contrast, with a very solid reality of its own. In reality, there are no such tangible, concrete objects. However, we have to ask, if these objects are unfindable, does this mean they do not exist at all? This is not the case. Of course they do exist. The question is not *whether* they exist but *how* they exist. They exist, but not in the manner in which we perceive them. They lack any discrete, intrinsic reality. This absence, or emptiness, of inherent existence is their ultimate nature.

The analytic process that seeks the true referents of our terms and concepts is not so complex, and it's not that difficult to arrive at the conclusion that things and events are unfindable when sought through such a process. However, this absence we arrive at after discerning the unfindability of phenomena through such analysis is not the final emptiness. Once we have arrived at this unfindability of things and events, then we can ask in what manner they actually do exist. We would then realize that the existence of things and events must be understood in terms of their relativity. And when we understand things and events as dependent for their existence on causes and conditions—and also as mere designations—we come to realize that things and events lack independence or self-determining authority. We see their nature clearly as dependent on other factors. And as long as anything exists only in dependence on other factors—governed by other forces—it cannot be said to be independent. For independence and dependence are mutually exclusive; there is also no third possibility.

It is critical to understand that a Madhyamika does not say that things are absent of inherent existence merely because they cannot be found when sought through critical analysis. This is not the full argument. Things and events are said to be absent of inherent or intrinsic existence because *they exist only in dependence on other factors*. This is the real premise. This style of reasoning eliminates two extremes—the extreme of nihilism, because one accepts a level of existence in terms of interdependence, and the extreme of absolutism, because one denies the intrinsic existence of phenomena.

The Buddha stated in sutra that anything that comes into being through dependence on conditions has the nature of being unborn. What does *unborn* mean here? Certainly we are not talking about the unborn nature of a nonexistent entity, such as the horn of a rabbit. Likewise, we are not denying the origination of things and events on a conventional level. What we are saying is that all phenomena that depend on conditions have the nature of emptiness. In other words, anything that depends on *other* factors is devoid of its own independent nature, and this absence of an independent nature is emptiness.

In his *Stanzas on the Fundamental Wisdom of the Middle Way,* Nagarjuna says that things and events, which are dependently originated, are empty, and thus are also dependently designated. He says dependent origination is the path of the Middle Way, which transcends the extremes of absolutism and nihilism. This statement is followed by another passage, which reads:

> There is no thing
> That is not dependently orginated;
> Therefore there is no thing
> That is not empty [of intrinsic existence].[17]

Nagarjuna concludes there is nothing that is not empty, for there is nothing that is not dependently originated. Here we see the equation between dependent origination and emptiness.

When we read the passages in *The Way of the Bodhisattva* dealing with the unfindability of things and events, it is crucial not to let ourselves be drawn into nihilism. This is the false conclusion that nothing really exists, and therefore, nothing really matters. This extreme must be avoided.

PRACTICING WISDOM

Beyond the Intellectual Understanding

An intellectual understanding of emptiness is different from a full realization of emptiness, wherein there is no cognition of the dependent origination of things. The Buddha states in a sutra cited in Nagarjuna's *Compendium of Sutras (Sutrasamuchaya)* that if in our meditations on emptiness we have even the slightest affirmative element—for instance, "This is emptiness," or "Things must exist"—then we are still caught in the web of grasping. As far as the cognitive content of our meditative experiences of emptiness is concerned, it must be a total absorption within the mere negation, the absence of intrinsic existence. There should be no affirmative elements within that meditative state.

However, when you have gained a very deep understanding of emptiness, you will get to a point where your very concept of existence and nonexistence changes. At this stage, even with regard to familiar objects, you will see a marked difference in your perception and your attitude toward them. You will recognize their illusion-like nature. That is, when the recognition dawns that although things appear to be solid and autonomous they do not exist in that way, this indicates that you are really arriving at an experiential understanding of emptiness. This is known as *perceiving things as illusion-like*. In fact, when you have gained a deep realization of emptiness, there is no need to make separate efforts to attain this perspective. After your own profound realization and experience of the emptiness of phenomena, things will appear spontaneously and naturally in the nature of illusion.

As your understanding of emptiness deepens and becomes a full experience of emptiness, you will be able to not only confirm the emptiness of phenomena by merely reflecting on dependent origination, but also your ascertainment of emptiness will reinforce your conviction in the validity of cause and effect. In this way, your understanding of both emptiness and dependent origination will reinforce and complement each other, giving rise to powerful progress in your realization.

You might think that when your understanding deepens in this way, you have reached such a high level of realization that you are at the threshold of becoming fully enlightened! This is definitely not the case. At this initial stage, on what is called the *path of accumulation,* your understanding of emptiness is still inferential. In deepening your understanding of emptiness further, it is essential to develop another mental factor—the faculty of single-pointedness. It is possible that we can, by using the analytic approach, arrive at a single-pointedness of the mind, but it is more effective and easier is to first have stability of the mind, and then, using that stability, reflect on the empty nature of phenomena. In any case, it is essential to attain tranquil abiding *(shamata)*. Once you have gained tranquil abiding, you then use that stable mind to meditate on emptiness. In this way you arrive at a union of tranquil abiding *(shamata)* and penetrative insight *(vipashyana)*.

You have now arrived at the *path of preparation*. From this point onward there will be a gradual reduction in dualistic appearances during meditative equipoise on emptiness. This gradual diminishing of dualistic appearances will culminate in a direct and utterly nonconceptual realization of emptiness. Such a state, free from dualism and grasping at intrinsic existence, is known as the *true path*. At this point, you have become an *arya,* a "superior being."

The true path results in the attainment of a true cessation—the cessation of certain levels of deluded states and afflictions. This is when we have an unmediated, experiential knowledge of the true Dharma, one of the three objects of refuge. Only at this stage do we really have the first opportunity to say "hello" to the true Dharma jewel. We have yet to tread the subsequent stages of the path in order to attain full enlightenment. During the first two paths of accumulation and preparation, the first incalculable eon of the accumulation of merit is completed. Through the first seven bodhisattva levels, which begin upon reaching the true path, the accumulation of merit of the second incalculable eon is completed. At the eighth bodhisattva level, we finally overcome all the afflictive emotions and thoughts. We then progress through the *pure grounds*—the eighth, ninth, and tenth bodhisattva levels—which are *pure* in that they are free from the stains of afflictions. It is during these three levels that the accumulation of merit of the third incalculable eon is perfected. So you can see that it takes a long time to attain complete enlightenment!

At the last instance of the tenth bodhisattva level, we generate an extremely powerful wisdom of emptiness that acts as an antidote to remove even the habitual patterns, predispositions, and imprints formed by all our past afflictions and deluded states of mind, and this then culminates in the attainment of full omniscience, or buddhahood.

The Crucial Sense of Commitment and Courage

We can see that there is a systematic "plan" for attaining enlightenment. You don't have to grope around in the dark without any direction. The layout of the entire path and its correlation to the accumulation of merit over a period of these incalculable eons illustrate a clear direction. Practitioners need to be aware of this fact and on that basis try to develop a deep determination and commitment to their spiritual pursuits. If you then supplement your practice with tantric Vajrayana methods, your approach will definitely be sound and well grounded.

If, on the other hand, when thinking of three incalculable eons, you become totally disheartened and discouraged and then try to seek an easier path for yourself through tantric practice, that's a totally wrong attitude. Furthermore, this would reflect that your commitment to Dharma practice is not strong. What is crucial is a sense of commitment and courage that is prepared—if necessary—to go through three incalculable eons to perfect the conditions for full enlightenment. If on the basis of such determination and courage you then embark on the Vajrayana path, your approach would be well grounded and powerful. Otherwise, it is like building a large structure without a firm foundation. Without doubt, there is great profundity in the tantric approach. However, whether that can be utilized depends on the capacity of the individual.

Of course, I am speaking here on the basis of my own personal observation. I too used to feel that three incalculable eons was too long. This time frame seemed unimaginable, something that I could not accept, whereas the time frame envisioned for enlightenment in tantra seemed more manageable. Understandably the swiftness of the Vajrayana path held a particular attraction. However, gradually my feelings have changed, especially toward the time frame of three incalculable eons. I have slowly grown to feel attracted toward the sutra approach and have actually begun to see the tremendous beneficial effects it can have in deepening our dedication to spiritual practice.

COMMENTARY

Mindfulness of the Emptiness of Feelings

Next is the meditation on the mindfulness of feelings, which Shantideva presents by analyzing the emptiness of feelings. We read the following:

88. If suffering itself is truly real,
Then why is joy not altogether quenched thereby?
If pleasure's real, then why will pleasant tastes
Not comfort and amuse a man in agony?

89. If the feeling fails to be experienced
Through being overwhelmed by something stronger,
How can "feeling" rightly be ascribed
To that which lacks the character of being felt?

90. Perhaps you say that only subtle pain remains,
Its grosser form has now been overmastered,
Or rather it is felt as mere pleasure.
But what is subtle still remains itself.

91. If, through presence of its opposite,
Pain and sorrow fail to manifest,
To claim with such conviction that it's felt
Is surely nothing more than empty words.

If the sensations of suffering and pain existed independently, they would not depend on other factors, and joyful experiences would be impossible. Similarly, if happiness existed independently, it would preclude grief, pain, and illness. And if the sensations of joy and pleasure existed intrinsically, then even were a person confronting an agonizing tragedy or pain, that person would still derive the same pleasure from food and comforts that he or she normally does.

Since feeling is in the nature of sensation, it must exist in relation to circumstances. We also find in our personal experiences that sensations can overwhelm one another. For example, if we are gripped by strong grief, that can permeate our entire experience and prevent us from experiencing any joy. Similarly, if we feel intense joy, that too can permeate our experience such that adverse news and mishaps do not cause us serious concern.

However, if we were to insist that underlying all of this is an independent event called *feeling,* the Madhyamika would respond, "Wouldn't that event depend on other factors, such as its causes and conditions?" So the idea of an independent feeling is only a fiction, a fantasy. There is no independently existing feeling that is not in the nature of pleasure, pain, or neutrality. There cannot be sensation or feeling that is not in the nature of any of these three basic patterns of experience.

Having established the absence of intrinsic existence of phenomena, Shantideva goes on to say that we should use this understanding as an antidote to our grasping at true existence—in this particular case, our grasping at feelings as if they have an independent, concrete reality.

92. Since so it is, the antidote
Is meditation and analysis.

Investigation and resultant concentration
Is indeed the food and sustenance of yogis.

Such single-pointed meditation on the emptiness of feeling is like the fuel for generating penetrative insight into emptiness. At the beginning of this ninth chapter, Shantideva stated that first we must cultivate single-pointedness of mind and attain tranquil abiding, and then generate penetrative insight. Through the combination of tranquil abiding and penetrative insight, the meditator will be able to engage in the profound yoga focused on emptiness. "The food and sustenance of yogis" refers to meditative absorption arrived at through contemplation on the emptiness of feelings.

Feelings, then, arise due to contact, which is their cause.

93. If between the sense power and a thing
There is a space, how will the two terms meet?
If there is no space, they form a unity,
And therefore, what is it that meets with what?

However, if sought through critical analysis, the contact that gives rise to feelings does not exist in any absolute sense either. This verse presents an analysis of the nature of contact. *Contact,* a mental factor, is defined as the meeting point between a sense faculty and an object. It arises when consciousness, the object, and the sense faculty all come together. Shantideva asks, "If there is an interval of space between the sense organs and sensory objects, where is the contact?" For example, if two atoms are totally intermingled, then they become identical; we cannot speak of a distinction between the two. So we read in the following verses:

94. Atoms and atoms cannot interpenetrate,
For they are equal, lacking any volume.
But if they do not penetrate, they do not mingle;
And if they do not mingle, there is no encounter.

95. For how could anyone accept
That what is partless could be said to meet?
And you must show me, if you ever saw,
A contact taking place between two partless things.

Not only that, Shantideva continues, but also, since consciousness is immaterial, how can we define it with the word *contact,* which relates to matter? "What can come into contact with consciousness?" he asks:

96. The consciousness is immaterial,
And so one cannot speak of contact with it.
A combination, too, has no reality,
And this we have already demonstrated.

97. Therefore, if there is no touch or contact,
Whence is it that feeling takes its rise?
What purpose is there, then, in all our striving,
What is it, then, that torments what?

Who could be harmed by painful experiences, since there is no such thing as intrinsically and absolutely existing painful sensations? Therefore, by examining contact—the cause of sensation—and by examining the nature of sensation itself, we find no intrinsically real sensation or feeling. The conclusion is that these exist only in dependence on other factors, and that nothing whatsoever can exist independently and intrinsically.

Through such analysis, we arrive at the important conclusion that neither the experiencer nor its object—the feeling—is truly existent. Once we have recognized this truth, the next logical step is to avert craving. This is presented in the following verse:

98. Since there is no subject for sensation,
And sensation, too, lacks all existence,
Why, when this you clearly understand,
Will you not pause and turn away from craving?

Furthermore, says Shantideva, when we think of the nature of sensation, what grounds do we have to claim that an independently existing feeling or sensation arises? The consciousness, or mind, that is simultaneous to the sensation cannot perceive such an autonomously real sensation.

99. Seeing, then, and sense of touch
Are stuff of insubstantial dreams.
If perceiving consciousness arises simultaneously,
How could such a feeling be perceived?

100. If the one arises first, the other after,
Memory occurs and not direct sensation.
Sensation, then, does not perceive itself,
And likewise, by another it is not perceived.

101. The subject of sensation has no real existence,
Thus sensation, likewise, has no being.
What damage, then, can be inflicted
On this aggregate deprived of self?

Nor can the moments of consciousness that precede and succeed the sensation perceive that sensation. The preceding moments are no longer present and remain only as imprints at the time of the sensation. And during the subsequent moments of consciousness the sensation remains only an object of recollection. Furthermore, there is no experiencer of the sensation as such. The conclusion we draw from this is that there is no sensation or feeling with independent reality. This completes the meditation on the mindfulness of feelings.

Mindfulness on the Emptiness of Mind

Next comes the meditation on the mindfulness of mind. It begins with the negation of any independent or intrinsic reality of mental consciousness.

102. The mind within the senses does not dwell;
It has no place in outer things, like form,
And in between, the mind does not abide:
Not out, not in, not elsewhere can the mind be found.

103. Something not within the body, and yet nowhere else,
That does not merge with it nor stand apart—
Something such as this does not exist, not even slightly.
Beings have nirvana by their nature.

The mind cannot exist within the body, as the body, or somewhere in between; nor can the mind exist independently of the body. Such a mind is not to be found; the mind is therefore devoid of intrinsic existence. And when beings recognize this nature of their mind, liberation can take place.

Although we know that consciousness exists, if we analyze and try to locate it within earlier or later moments of its continuum, the idea of consciousness as a unitary entity begins to disappear, just as with the analysis of the body. Through such analysis we arrive at the absence of intrinsic existence of consciousness. This applies equally to sensory experiences, such as visual perceptions, as they also share the same nature.

104. If consciousness precedes the cognized object,
With regard to what does it arise?
If consciousness arises with its object,
Again, regarding what does it arise?

105ab. If consciousness comes later than its object,
Once again, from what does it arise?

If a consciousness, such as a sensory perception, arises simultaneously with its object, then they cannot be maintained as sequential—that is, the object exists and then consciousness cognizes it. If they were simultaneous, how could an object give rise to a cognition?

If, on the other hand, the object exists first and then consciousness of it comes later, cognition comes only after the cessation of the object. If this were the case, what would that cognition be aware of, for the object has ceased to exist? When we subject sensory perceptions to this kind of critical analysis, they too are revealed to be unfindable, just as in the case of mental consciousness.

Mindfulness of the Emptiness of All Phenomena

105cd. Thus the origin of all phenomena
Lies beyond the reach of understanding.

Generally, the argument used to establish the substantial reality of phenomena is that things and events have functions, where specific conditions give rise to certain things and particular circumstances lead to particular events. So we assume that things and events must be real, that they must have substantial reality. This principle of functionality is the key premise the Realists use in asserting the independent existence of things and events. If the Madhyamika is successful in negating the intrinsic existence of these functional entities, then—as Nagarjuna put it in *Stanzas on the Fundamental Wisdom of the Middle Way*—it becomes easier to negate the intrinsic existence of more abstract entities, such as space and time.

Many of these arguments seem to use the principles of the Madhyamaka reasoning known as *the absence of identity and difference*. For example, the divisible and composite nature of material phenomena is explained in terms of directional parts. In the case of consciousness, its composite nature is explained mainly from the point of view of its continuum of moments. With regard to such abstract entities as space and time, we can understand their composite nature in terms of their directions. So, as long as a thing is divisible—as long as we can break it into composite parts—we can establish its nature as dependent upon its parts. If, on the other hand, a thing were to exist intrinsically as a substantial reality, then that thing would not be dependent upon its parts; it would instead exist as an indivisible and completely discrete entity.

MEDITATION

Meditate now according to your individual choice. You may wish to meditate on emptiness, on impermanence, or on suffering.

10. COUNTERING OBJECTIONS

PRACTICING WISDOM

Dualistic Elaborations

At the beginning of his *Stanzas on the Fundamental Wisdom of the Middle Way,* Nagarjuna pays homage to Buddha Shakyamuni. The manner in which he extols the Buddha's virtues and pays homage to him outlines his two main themes—the teaching of emptiness and the principle of dependent origination. In two verses, Nagarjuna salutes the Buddha as someone who has the capacity to teach the philosophy of emptiness and dependent origination with authority and with full knowledge of the appropriate timing, and of the spiritual needs, mental capacities, and temperaments of his listeners.

In these two verses he states that dependently originated phenomena—things and events—possess characteristics such as origination, cessation, and mobility. In terms of characteristics, there are such qualities as origination and cessation. In terms of time, there are existence and nonexistence, as well as mobility—going and coming. In terms of identity, there are oneness and multiplicity. All of these characteristics exist on the conventional level. These characteristics do not inhere in things and events as their ultimate natures. From the ultimate perspective of the direct realization of emptiness, these diverse characteristics do not exist.

Emptiness is described by Nagarjuna as the total dissolution of all dualistic elaborations. When we speak of dualistic elaborations, there are of course different meanings. For instance, it could mean the elaboration of substantial reality, which is the object to be negated—such a dualistic elaboration does not even exist conventionally. Dualistic elaboration sometimes also refers to the ignorant mind grasping onto true existence and its derivative deluded states of mind. When dualistic elaborations are understood this way, although they are objects to be refuted, they do exist conventionally.

Sometimes, dualistic elaboration also refers to conventional characteristics, such as the eight characteristics of dependently originated phenomena—origination, cessation, and so on. From the perspective of direct realization of emptiness, these elaborations do not exist because they are not the ultimate nature of the reality. It is by the nonseeing and nonperceiving of these characteristics that the arya being, in meditative equipoise, is said to realize emptiness directly. That does not mean, however, that these characteristics of phenomena are to be negated, nor does it mean that these characteristics do not exist conventionally. They are not perceived by the meditator in his meditative equipoise when the mind is totally fused, single-pointedly and directly, with the realization of emptiness. However, they *do* conventionally inhere in dependently originated phenomena.

Therefore, we need to distinguish between emptiness, which is the ultimate nature of reality, and *being in the nature of* emptiness. For example, conventional phenomena, such as things and events, cannot be said to be emptiness as such, but are rather in the nature of emptiness in that they are empty of intrinsic existence. From the perspective of the meditative equipoise that perceives emptiness directly and is totally fused with that realization, conventional phenomena do not exist because they are not perceptible to someone in that meditative equipoise.

Nagarjuna states in *Stanzas on the Fundamental Wisdom of the Middle Way* that by realizing emptiness, we can cease the dualistic and conceptual elaborations constructed by karma and afflictions. He states that when karma and afflictions cease, one attains nirvana, freedom. So nirvana is defined in terms of the cessation karma and afflictions, a state where afflictions have completely come to an end and where karma has lost its potency to produce rebirths. The individual may still carry karmic imprints but can no longer create new karma, because the afflictions, which give rise to karma, have been eliminated. Dharmakirti helps us understand this further when he states in his *Valid Cognition* that within the psyche of the being who has gone beyond the ocean of samsara, karmic imprints can still be found. However, these imprints cannot give rise to future rebirths in cyclic existence because the cooperative conditions, the afflictions, have been totally eliminated.

How does such a nirvana or freedom come about? There are four factors—karma, afflictions, conceptual thought processes, and dualistic elaborations, the cessation of which is related to this question. Karma is created by afflictions, afflictions are created by conceptual thought processes, and the conceptual thought processes are fueled by dualistic elaborations, which here refers to the ignorant mind grasping onto the true existence of phenomena. Therefore, the causes giving rise to rebirth in cyclic existence are karma and afflictions. Grasping onto true existence can only be eliminated by generating insight into emptiness. So, only by generating the awareness that penetrates the nature of emptiness can the dualistic elaboration grasping onto true existence of phenomena be eliminated.

The Ultimate Creator

Khunu Rinpoche states that there can be a different reading of the line about the pacification of dualistic elaborations in *Stanzas on the Fundamental Wisdom of the Middle Way*. He says it can be read as stating that not only is it the insight into emptiness that eliminates the dualistic elaborations, but also it is within the sphere of emptiness that dualistic elaborations are ultimately pacified. So now, when Nagarjuna speaks of pacification of afflictions within the sphere of emptiness, what is meant by *emptiness* here? Emptiness should not be viewed as a kind of ontological category, existing "out there" and separate from the particular things and events. In the context of Nagarjuna's verse, *emptiness* refers specifically to the emptiness of the mind—the mind's absence of independent, intrinsic existence. In this context, we can say then that the ultimate creator of all phenomena, both samsara and nirvana, is the mind. All the afflictions and delusions of mind that are created by mind must finally be cleansed by the nature of the mind itself. In other words, the mental pollutions and so on that are created by the mind must be eliminated by utilizing methods that are rooted in the mind. The result—the fully enlightened state of buddhahood—is also a state of mind. So what we find here is that the mind plays a tremendously important role in our process of purification and perfection. It says in the *Sublime Continuum (Uttaratantra)* that all pollutants of the mind are adventitious; that is, they are separable from the mind. And all the enlightened qualities of the Buddha's omniscient mind exist as potentials in the minds of sentient beings.

In Sakya literature, there is a statement that within the basis, which is the causal *mind-basis-of-all (kun shi),* all phenomena of samsara and nirvana are complete. Thus the mind-basis-of-all is in some sense the fundamental innate mind of clear light. All phenomena of samsara exist within that basis. This is at the level of ordinary beings, not where the individual has become perfected. Therefore, this foundational consciousness is called the *causal continuum*. Within that causal continuum, all phenomena of samsara are complete in the form of their natural characteristics, all phenomena of the paths and grounds are complete in the form of their qualities, and all enlightened qualities of the Buddha's omniscient mind are complete in the form of their potentials. This summarizes the essence of the Sakya approach to the understanding of the grounds, path, and result. It presents a beautiful and comprehensive picture.

Therefore, whether it is the Nyingmapas' *dzokchen,* the *mahamudra* of the Kagyu school, the Sakyas' *lamdré* view of the union of profundity and clarity, or the Gelug understanding of *mind isolation* according to the *Guhyasamaja Tantra,* the emphasis is on realizing the ultimate nature of mind. When it comes to emptiness, of course, there is no difference between the mind's emptiness and the emptiness of external objects. Contemplation on the emptiness of mind is especially emphasized in meditative practices in all four schools of Tibetan Buddhism because of it has such a dramatic impact on the mind of the practitioner.

When I refer to *mind* in this context, I am using the term in a general sense, without distinguishing between *sem* (mind) and *rikpa* (pristine awareness). I am using *mind* as a general term covering all types of cognitive events. The main point I am making is that when talking of the cessation of conceptual or dualistic elaborations, it is important to be aware of the different meanings of the expression according to the different contexts. For example, among dualistic elaborations, some can be negated and some cannot; some exist and some do not. We need to be sensitive to how context affects the meaning of terminology.

COMMENTARY

Defending the Two Truths

In the last chapter we saw Shantideva defend the Madhyamaka philosophy of emptiness against criticisms by explaining the nature of the existence of phenomena. His opponent now asserts that according to the Madhyamaka view, it would be impossible to establish the two truths. As for the division of the root text in this section, the commentaries of Minyak Künsö and Khenpo Künpal both agree. However, there appears to be a slight difference in their reading of the relevant verses. I will first present Minyak Künsö's reading.

In these first two verses, the opponent argues that because the Madhyamikas claim that all phenomena are devoid of inherent existence, they cannot speak coherently of identity or even existence.

106. "If this is so," you say, "the relative will cease,
And then the two truths—what becomes of them?
If relative depends on beings' minds,
This means nirvana is attained by none."

107. This relative is just the thoughts of beings;
That is not the relative of beings in nirvana.
If thoughts come after this, then that is still the relative;
If not, the relative has truly ceased.

If all phenomena lack inherent existence, objects Shantideva's opponent, then all conventional realities—things and events—will be devoid of identities. If this is so, conventional reality will cease to exist. And if conventional reality does not exist, then even ultimate truth cannot exist. So, how can you maintain that there are two truths?

This doubt arises from misunderstanding what is meant by conventional truth. Earlier I mentioned that in the context of conventional truth—and from the perspective of a misperceiving mind—reality is understood in terms of things and events having some form of objective truth. This is analogous to mistakenly perceiving a snake when seeing a coiled rope. There is no basis in reality for such a perception to be valid. Similarly, nothing in reality—whether a thing or an event—exists substantially, inherently, or independently in its own right. To this the opponent raises the objection that nothing would exist if no thing or event exists in its own right. And if that is so, they continue, how can you Madhyamikas maintain that sentient beings can attain freedom?

The Madhyamikas respond by stating that conventional truth is posited in relation to the perspectives of sentient beings. The everyday world of conventional truth is said to be true from the perspective of the ignorant mind that apprehends things and events as having inherent existence. But that perspective is invalid. However, within conventional terms, there is a perspective where the existence of things and events can be established as valid.

Conventional realities have the power to affect our lives—they cause pain and pleasure, for example. The question can be asked, "What exactly are the Prasangika-Madhyamaka criteria for establishing things and events as conventionally real or existent?" There are three criteria, and they hinge upon the understanding that only in the aftermath of negating the intrinsic existence of things and events can we validly and coherently establish their conventional reality. The first criterion states that things and events are validly established by valid experience or convention. The second states that the truth of their existence cannot be contravened by valid experiences. And the third states that conventional realities cannot be negated by analysis into their ultimate nature.

This is utterly different from an illusion, where we perceive an object on the basis of something else. For example, in a magic trick, we might see illusory horses and elephants because of the magician's conjuring powers. The horses and elephants are, even in conventional terms, false perceptions. Therefore, the perception of horses and elephants can be invalidated by other valid experiences. One need not resort to an ultimate analysis to disprove them. Given these two types of conventional perceptions—one valid and the other false—it is critical to be able to distinguish between, say, a real person and a dream person. For example, one distinction between slaying a real person and taking the life of a dream person is that in one case, a cardinal nonvirtue is committed, while in the other case this is not so. But while a dream person is not a real person, both are equal in lacking intrinsic existence. It is therefore important to be able to maintain a coherent approach to conventional reality in the aftermath of negating intrinsic existence.

Khenpo Künpal, however, reads these verses as relating to the perspective of the fully enlightened mind. He says that if, following the attainment of full enlightenment—which is characterized as the total dissolution of all conceptual elaborations—the reality of conventional phenomena is not maintained, then things, events, and their conventions will not be real.

By meditating on the sphere wherein all dualistic elaborations have been pacified, we accumulate wisdom. And we accumulate merit by deepening our conviction in the validity of the causal principles within the context of conventional truth. It is only on the path that combines these two elements—the accumulation of both merit and wisdom—that we can make our way to the Buddha's full enlightenment.

As this next verse suggests, categories such as "subject and object," "perception and object," "one and many," "self and others," and of course, the "existence of all phenomena" are dependent upon worldly conventions. They are thus relative.

108. Analysis and what is to be analyzed
Are linked together, mutually dependent.
It is on the basis of conventional consensus
That all examination is expressed.

Now, a further objection is raised by the opponent:

109. "But when the process of analysis
Is made in turn the object of our scrutiny,
This investigation, likewise, may be analyzed,
And thus we find an infinite regress."

They contend that if it is through the application of critical analysis that we examine the ultimate nature of phenomena, then the analysis itself is also ultimately subject to such critical analysis. In this analysis then, another analyzing mind is needed, which in turn would require another analysis, and so on, leading to an infinite regress. Shantideva presents the Madhyamika's response to this objection:

110. If phenomena are truly analyzed,
No basis for analysis remains.
Deprived of further object, it subsides.
That indeed is said to be nirvana.

When the object of an inquiry is subjected to critical analysis, the subject too is revealed to be devoid of any intrinsic reality or intrinsic origination. This absence is described as nirvana, the state beyond sorrow. So while a meditator is directly experiencing the emptiness of intrinsic existence of all phenomena, there is no basis for grasping onto the intrinsic existence of anything else. For the meditator in this state, there is no awareness of subject and object. A subject–object distinction could be made, but since the meditator's mind is totally fused with the absence of inherent existence, there is no need to analyze the emptiness of the analyzing mind itself.

Above, we discussed the many different subtleties of emptiness or selflessness. When a person has an awareness of the grosser levels of emptiness, it is possible that, within the psyche of the individual, notions of self-existence corresponding to subtler levels of emptiness still persist. However, if you experience subtle emptiness—such as the emptiness of inherent existence as understood by the Prasangika-Madhyamaka school—then while that ascertainment remains manifest in your mind, there is no room for any grasping onto any degree of selfhood or self-existence to arise.

Countering the Buddhist Realists

In the next section, Shantideva refutes the conceptions of true existence by various schools of thought. He begins with the analysis of the positions of the Buddhist realists—the Vaibhashikas and Sautrantikas—who state that sensory perceptions—visual perceptions and so forth—and their objects both possess intrinsic or substantial reality. These views are negated in the following verses.

111. Those who say that "both are true"
Are hard pressed to maintain their case.
If consciousness reveals the truth of things,
By what support is consciousness upheld?

112. If objects show that consciousness exists,
What, in turn, upholds the truth of objects?
If both subsist through mutual dependence,
Both thereby will lose their true existence.

The realists maintain that both subject and object possess real and substantial existence. The Madhyamikas, however, object by pointing out the logical inconsistencies and flawed reasoning behind such a philosophical view. The Madhyamika asks, "If consciousness establishes the substantial reality of things, then what support do you have to claim the substantial reality of the subject—consciousness itself? However, if objects validate the substantial reality of the subject—consciousness—then what validates the substantial reality of the object? If subject and object are established by means of mutual dependence—certifying each others' substantial reality—then both lose their substantial reality. For were they substantially and intrinsically real, they would be independent of each other." The Madhyamika then uses an analogy to demonstrate that subject and object are mutually dependent and neither enjoys any independent, substantial existence:

113. If, without a son, a man can not be a father;
Whence, indeed, will such a son arise?
There is no father in the absence of a son.
Just so, the mind and object have no true existence.

In this next verse, a further defense by the opponent is anticipated by Shantideva.

114. "The plant arises from the seed," you say,
"So why should not the seed be thence inferred?

Consciousness arises from the object—
How does it not show the thing's existence?"

The opponent argues that a shoot indicates the presence of a seed. Indeed, this is a basic premise of the realists, who assert the substantial reality of the origination of things and events. By analogy, then, they argue, since consciousness arises from the object, how does it not indicate the real existence of the object?

The Madhyamaka responds that a subject, or consciousness, distinct from the shoot is needed to deduce the existence of the seed.

115. A consciousness that's different from the plant itself
Deduces the existence of the seed.
But what will show that consciousness exists,
Whereby the object is itself established?

By what means do we cognize the existence of consciousness? What is being demonstrated here is that subject and object are mutually dependent, and thus neither enjoys independent, autonomous status. Therefore, neither cognition nor its object possesses intrinsic existence. They are both relative.

PRACTICING WISDOM

The Importance of Reason

Aryadeva mentions in *Four Hundred Verses on the Middle Way* that if we trace the origin of material things, we find that their continuum is beginningless. Material things can have an end, but in terms of their continuum they are beginningless. Whether it be the external environment of rocks and plants and so on or the sentient beings living in it, if we were to trace their material origin, we could trace it to the beginning of our universe.

According to the *Kalachakra Tantra,* matter can be traced back to a point when all matter was space particles. A particular universe system comes into being, remains for a long time, and then dissolves into an empty space. And from that empty space an entire world again emerges through a process of evolution. From the Buddhist point of view, there is a repetitive cycle of evolution and dissolution of the physical universe. This process seems to have some parallels with contemporary scientific explanations of our cosmos.

If we compare modern cosmology's description of Earth—its size, shape, age, and distance from other planets—with Buddhist texts such as the *Treasury of Higher Knowledge (Abhidharmakosha),* which also presents cosmology, we find many contradictions. The Abhidharma cosmology seems to conflict with the scientific account derived from empirical observation. As Buddhists who accept the principle of reason, we must accept that these Abhidharma views contradict valid knowledge. The only option open to us here, therefore, is to discard Abhidharma cosmology as an accurate description of the physical universe and accept the scientific account.

In Mahayana Buddhism there is a hermeneutical tradition known as the *four reliances*. The first reliance says that we should rely not on the person but rather on his or her work; second, regarding that work, we should not rely on the words but rather on the meaning; third, with respect to meaning, we should rely not on the provisional but rather the definitive meaning; and fourth, with regard to the definitive meaning, we should rely not on mere intellectual knowledge but rather on experiential understanding.

The upshot is that any statement or claim that contradicts reason and valid experience cannot be upheld. Therefore, as Buddhists, we must discard any tenet that may contradict reason and valid experience. This is the general methodology in Buddhism—particularly in Mahayana thought. However, it is important to draw a distinction between the non-observance of something and the observance of its nonexistence. Disproving something and not being able to prove something are two different things. This is a critical distinction.

From the perspective of ordinary beings, there are three categories of phenomena—the apparent, the slightly obscure, and the extremely obscure. Cognition of apparent phenomena requires no reasoning, the cognition of slightly obscure phenomena is arrived at by inference, and extremely obscure phenomena can only be fully known on the basis of scriptural authority. The emptiness of intrinsic existence of all things is an example of the second category—the slightly obscure. It is not evident to us, and we need to rely on reasoned inferences to arrive at an understanding of it.

This threefold classification is not absolute. Some of the Buddhist concepts, such as the nature of the form and formless realms, or the fact that an individual's path to enlightenment requires three innumerable eons, are extremely obscure to us. They are neither apparent to us nor can they be known fully through reasoning. At our present level of consciousness, the only means available to us is the testimony of another person. However, from the Buddhist point of view, the testimony of another person cannot be taken as an authority simply because the person happens to be holy or well known. So how do we determine the validity of a person's testimony? We need to subject that person's words to analysis, examining whether that person's descriptions of apparent phenomena contradict our valid experience, and whether that person's explanations of slightly obscure phenomena are affirmed or denied by logical inference. Once we have gained confidence in that person's reliability in these first two categories of phenomena, then we examine what that person says about extremely obscure phenomena. We can check to see whether there are inconsistencies between the earlier and the later propositions and between the explicit and implicit standpoints. Although the propositions may remain extremely obscure to us—that is, we have no direct or logical means by which to test their validity, either proving or disproving them—we can take the speaker's testimony as authoritative since his or her words have been proven valid in the areas where the propositions have allowed for logical analysis.

Karma and Causality

Earlier we spoke about causality, the relationship between cause and effect, and at what stage the karma of sentient beings affects the causal process. I feel that there is a causal process that is the general law of causation and also a stage where the intention of a sentient being can set a new chain of causal processes in motion. However, identifying this stage, I think, is extremely difficult, if not impossible.

So how exactly can we understand the karmic continuum? To give an example, when a stick is burned, although the wood has disappeared, it remains in the form of energy; it has not disappeared completely. The Prasangika-Madhyamaka school adopts a similar notion of *cessation (shik pa)*. This view maintains that although the physical reality of a phenomenon ceases, it remains as a type of energy or a potential. Other Buddhist philosophical schools accept this cessation to be merely a mental construct or an abstract entity. In contrast, Prasangika-Madhyamikas consider this as a type of potential, having the capacity to become a future cause within that continuum. I feel that the scientific idea of conservation of energy is in some ways similar to this notion of cessation.

Cessation as a kind of potential refers to the point when the physical reality of an object has become nonexistent, but a potential still remains that can affect the course of the continuum of that object. This is, of course, different from the *cessation* of mental obscurations at nirvana. For while in both cessations something has ended, in the state of nirvana, the potential is no longer there. No new mental obscurations can arise.

Within the twelve links of dependent origination, the second, *volition,* is karma, and the tenth, *becoming,* also belongs to the category of karma. However, this does not mean that the karma of the second link has suddenly resurfaced. Rather, the potential implanted by the karmic action has reached a point where it has become fully activated and is ready to give rise to its fruition. So here we are referring to a potential that was left by the execution of a karmic act.

MEDITATION

For this meditation, focus on compassion. It is not enough merely to develop the wish that all sentient beings be free from suffering. Since sentient beings do not have the capacity to totally overcome their sufferings on their own, you should, on your part, develop a deep commitment to take responsibility to help all beings overcome suffering. This meditation is an excellent preparation for the generation of bodhichitta, the altruistic intention to attain buddhahood for the benefit of all beings.

11. KEY ARGUMENTS REFUTING INTRINSIC EXISTENCE

COMMENTARY

In the next subsection, verses 116–50, Shantideva presents various arguments for refuting inherent existence, such as the diamond splinters argument, the argument of identity and difference, the reasoning of interdependent origination, and the reasoning of existence and nonexistence.

The diamond splinters argument refutes the inherent existence of phenomena by examining causation with a fourfold analysis. The argument of identity and difference negates the inherent existence of phenomena by examining their essential natures. This argument can be further elaborated into different forms, such as the fivefold reasoning and sevenfold reasoning. The reasoning of existence and nonexistence analyzes the effects of things and events, examining whether those effects are existent or nonexistent. A further form of this argument that analyzes from the point of view of both cause and effect—asking whether one cause leads to many effects, or whether multiple causes lead to one effect. Finally, there is the reasoning of dependent origination, which is really the king of all reasoning.

The Diamond Splinters Argument

We begin with the reasoning of the diamond splinters. The text makes the observation that the conventional mind perceives through direct experience all sorts of causes. For example, the distinct parts of a lotus, such as its stalk, result from distinct causes.

116. At times direct perception of the world
Perceives that all things have their causes.
The different segments of the lotus flower
Arise from a similar diversity of causes.

117. "But what gives rise," you ask, "to such diversity of causes?"
An ever-earlier variety of cause, we say.
"And how," you ask, "do certain fruits derive from certain causes?"
Through the power, we answer, of preceding causes.

Generally speaking, the distinction between existent and nonexistent is made on the basis of whether something is established by a valid cognition. Within the category of existing things, some things come into being occasionally, and some are everpresent. The fact that something comes into being only occasionally indicates that a cause or a condition must have given rise to it, while an everpresent phenomenon does not appear to require such precedents. We can thus observe two principal classes of phenomena—those that depend on causes and conditions and those that do not. In addition, those occasional phenomena are by nature impermanent, and those phenomena that are always present are called permanent.

Whether it be the external environment or the sentient beings inhabiting it, they all come into being by depending on causes and conditions. They do not come into being causelessly. What then are their causes? Furthermore, the multiplicity of effects must correspond to their causes. In other words, diverse effects must have diverse causes. What gives rise to this multiplicity of causes? Shantideva presents the Madhyamika's response that a preceding variety of causes give rise to them. In other words, a multiplicity of causes comes about due to a multiplicity of earlier causes. The text then reads, "And how...do certain fruits derive from certain causes?" That is, what enables causes to produce certain types of effects? Again, the answer is that they are able to do this due to their preceding causes.

After refuting the notion—in the first part of the diamond splinters argument—that things and events could come into being without a cause, Shantideva next refutes the idea that things and events can come into being from a permanent cause. In the following verses, the candidates for a permanent original cause of the universe—such as the primal substance or *Ishvara,* the divine creator—are rejected.

118. If Ishvara is held to be the cause of beings,
You must now define for us his nature.
If, by this, you simply mean the elements,
No need to tire ourselves disputing names!

If, Shantideva argues, Ishvara is held to be the cause of beings, then the proponents of this argument must now define his nature. However, if by *Ishvara* you are simply referring to the elements, then, says Shantideva, even we Madhyamikas accept that elements are the causes and conditions of things and events. So why give it an exotic name like Ishvara? If Ishvara is identical to the elements, since there are multiple elements, then Ishvara too will become multiple, impermanent, inert—in other words, not divine.

119. Yet earth and other elements are many,
Impermanent, inert, without divinity.
Trampled underfoot, they are impure,
And thus they cannot be a God Omnipotent.

120. The Deity cannot be Space—inert and lifeless.
He cannot be the Self, for this we have refuted.
He's inconceivable, they say. Then likewise his
creatorship.
Is there any point, therefore, to such a claim?

121. What is it he wishes to create?
Has he made the self and all the elements?
But are not self and elements and he, himself, eternal?
And consciousness, we know, arises from its object.

And further, by being an element, Ishvara can be trampled upon. Ishvara would therefore be impure. How can that be God? Also, Ishvara cannot be said to be space because he would be inert and lifeless. Nor can he be said to be the self, which was refuted earlier. If we maintain that Ishvara is an inconceivable entity, then nothing could be said about it, and so, Shantideva asks, what point is there in making such claims? Furthermore, what is the wish of such a creator? Has he made the self and all the elements? Are not self and the elements Ishvara himself? Also, Shantideva points out, we know consciousness, for example, to arise from its object, not from Ishvara.

Shantideva now states the Madhyamika's own position—that pleasure and pain come about due to past karmic actions. So he asks the opponent, what exactly is created by Ishvara?

122. Pain and pleasure have, from all time, sprung
from karma,
So tell us, what has this Divinity produced?
And if creation's cause is unoriginate,
How can origin be part of the result?

123. Why are creatures not created constantly,
For Ishvara relies on nothing but himself?
And if there's nothing that he has not made,
What remains on which he might depend?

Because Ishvara is, according to the proponents of this idea, a permanent creator, he can have no beginning; therefore, cause has no beginning. If cause has no beginning, Shantideva is asking, how can effects have any beginning? Moreover, if the cause is permanent, how can we speak of it producing something? We cannot speak of a causal production, because in order for an effect to be produced by a cause, there needs to be a condition for the cause to exist. Since everything is created by Ishvara, how can Ishvara—the cause—depend upon conditions? If on the other hand, the creator Ishvara is dependent on conditions, then the effects—things and events—come into being through a combination of Ishvara and Ishvara's conditions. This destroys the thesis that all things and events are created by Ishvara as a single, solitary cause.

PRACTICING WISDOM

Two Kinds of Causation

I would like to take a few moments to explore further the connection between karmic and natural causation. As Shantideva has stated, the truth of the situation is that consciousness, or perception, arises in dependence upon an object by taking on the aspect of the particular object. Therefore, consciousness and perception arise in dependence upon objects. Consciousness, as far as its basic nature of luminosity and awareness is concerned, is beginningless. Every moment of consciousness is a result, or product, of its preceding moment—this continuum is beginningless. Sensations and experiences such as joy and pain are products of karma and action.

While experiences of pain and joy come about as a result of karma, all material phenomena come about due to their preceding substantial causes. As I mentioned earlier, there seem to be two causal processes working in parallel. On the one hand is the natural law of cause and effect, which is independent of karma. And when sentient beings' experience of pain and pleasure enters the picture, karma also enters. At that point, there seems to be a second level of natural, karmic law of cause and effect.

According to the tradition of upper Abhidharma, karma is defined as a mental event. However, the Prasangika-Madhyamika accepts physical, or bodily, karma as well. Generally karma must be understood in terms of action. In our everyday life, almost everything we experience comes about as a result of actions. Without action, there is no life. We act due to our natural aspiration to seek happiness and overcome suffering. One of the most critical elements of action is the motivation. When we take the factor of motivation into account, then the nature of action—whether positive, negative, or neutral, and to whatever degree—becomes a rather complex question. A state of mind motivated by an afflictive emotion gives rise to impulsive, often negative, actions, whether bodily or verbal, and these negative actions produce corresponding consequences. We can understand this from our daily experience—it is easily observable. Our existence as human beings is said to be the product of virtuous karma—meritorious actions accumulated in the past.

As far as the material continua of our human aggregates, or *skandhas,* is concerned—especially our physical aggregates—we can trace their origins even to the beginning of the present universe, and they should be there even at the point *before* the evolution of our current universe. So in terms of their continua, the aggregates are beginningless. As far as the causal relationship between the various stages of an inanimate material continuum is concerned, I do not think karma plays any role. That an earlier instant gives rise to a later instant by means of a normal, causal process is purely a function of a natural law. Many transformations of material substances happen as a result of elemental changes at the material level.

However, when we speak of an element that is part of an animate body, then I feel that it has some connection to karma. As far as the evolution or origination of an element itself is concerned, I do not think that has any connection with karma, but when an element has the capacity or potential to affect an individual sentient being's experience, I think karma does enter into the picture. From the point of view of Buddhist cosmology, before the evolution of the current universal system, *space particles* existed that gradually evolved through interaction into grosser physical matter, such as subatomic particles, atoms, and molecules. Vajrayana texts mention both external and internal elements. Internal elements are finally traced to the most refined elements, which are explained in terms of the *energy winds (pranas),* which flow through subtle physical channels. The texts also acknowledge an association between the external elements and the internal channels and winds. Perhaps it is at this level that we can locate the basis for the connection with karma.

If karma does indeed provide the connection between the external and internal elements, then on this basis, we may be able to account for how inert material substances later become animate enough to serve as the basis for consciousness and sensations. I feel that it is through the understanding of this idea of the subtle energy winds found in the Vajrayana texts that we can possibly find a link between karma and the material world. This is, of course, the speculation of an individual. It is nothing conclusive.

COMMENTARY

Continuing the Diamond Splinters Argument

Next Shantideva explains that if the aggregation of causes and conditions is the cause of things and events, then the idea of Ishvara being the cause loses its coherence, for when causes and conditions come into being and are aggregated, no other force can prevent the fruition of the results. Even Ishvara would have to depend on the aggregation to be able to produce anything.

124. If Ishvara depends, the cause of all
Is prior circumstances, and no longer he.

When these obtain, he cannot but create;
When these are absent, he is powerless to make.

125. If almighty God does not intend,
But yet creates, another thing has forced him.
If he wishes to create he's swayed by his desire.
Even though Creator, then, what comes of his
omnipotence?

Furthermore, if Ishvara acts without desiring to act—in other words, is forced—it would follow that he is under the control of something else. Even if Ishvara acts with the desire to act, then he would be conditioned by desire. In that case, what remains of the concept of a divinity, a creator, or a single unitary cause?

The Vaisheshikas hold that permanent, indivisible atoms are the foundations, or creators, of the physical universe. So first Shantideva briefly turns his attention to this notion, and says that this view was refuted earlier.

126. Those who say that atoms are the permanent
foundation
Have indeed already been refuted.
The Samkhyas are the ones who hold
The Primal Substance as enduring cause.

127. "Pleasure," "pain," "neutrality," so-called,
Are qualities that, when they rest
In equilibrium, are termed the Primal Substance.
The universe arises when they are disturbed.

128. Three natures in a unity are disallowed;
This unity, therefore, cannot exist.
These qualities, likewise, have no existence,
For they must also be assigned a triple nature.

129. If these qualities have no existence,
A thing like sound is very far from plausible!
And cloth, and other mindless objects,
Cannot be the seat of feelings such as pleasure.

Then he turns to the views of the Samkhya school, in particular its concept of *primal substance* as the basic creator of the entire universe. The Samkhyas define *primal substance* as the state of equilibrium of three forces—goodness, passion, and darkness—and assert it to be the underlying cause or foundation of the entire physical universe. Shantideva refutes this notion by stating that if the primal substance were a single, unitary entity, we could not define it as an equilibrium of three qualities. This would contradict the Samkhyas' own tenets, according to which even these three qualities are said to be composed of three further qualities. Therefore, Shantideva argues, in the final analysis, a coherent notion of a unitary, single entity cannot be sustained. Also, in the Samkhya view, pain, pleasure, and neutrality ultimately become permanent. However, given that they are states of feeling, how can they be permanent? How can something permanent be described in terms of sensations or states of feeling, which are observably fleeting?

Next Shantideva addresses the Samkhyas' view that everything exists at their causal stage:

130. "But," you say, "these things possess the nature
of their cause."
But have we not investigated "things" already?
For you the cause is pleasure and the like,
But from pleasure, cloth has never sprung!

131. Pleasure, rather, is produced from cloth,
But this is nonexistent, therefore pleasure likewise.
As for permanence of pleasure and the rest—
Well, there's a thing that's never been observed.

Shantideva rejects this assertion by stating that it contradicts our direct experience, which affirms the sequential process of the arising of cause and effect. The causal stage is when the effect has not yet come into being, and the effect stage is when the cause has already ceased to exist. Therefore, Shantideva concludes that in the Samkhya view of primal substance, the very concept of cause and effect and their sequential order becomes untenable.

In the following verses, Shantideva rejects pleasure, pain, and the sensations as being truly existent.

132. If pleasure and the rest are true existents,
Why are they not constantly perceived?
And if you claim they take on subtle form,
How can coarseness change, transforming into subtlety?

133. If coarseness is abandoned, subtlety assumed,
Such transition indicates impermanence.
Why then not accept that, in this way,
All things will have the character of transience?

134. If you say the coarser aspect is itself the pleasure,
The manifest sensation is of course impermanent.
And what does not exist in any sense,
Because it has no being, cannot manifest.

135. You do not intend that what is manifest
Lacked earlier existence—yet this is the meaning.
And if results exist within their cause,
Those who eat their food, consume their excrement.

136. And likewise with the money they would spend on clothing,
Let them rather buy the cotton grain to wear.
"But," you say, "the world is ignorant and blind."
Since this is taught by those who know the truth,

137. This knowledge must be present in the worldly.
And if they have it, why do they not see?
You say, "The views of worldly folk are false."
Therefore, what they clearly see has no validity.

In the following verse Shantideva presents a possible objection to the Madhyamikas from the Samkhyas' standpoint:

138. "But if there is no truth in their cognition,
All that it assesses is perforce deceptive.
Meditation on the supreme truth of emptiness
Ceases, therefore, to have any meaning."

The Samkhyas could assert that the Madhyamaka position appears to accept different types of valid cognitions, such as direct perception and inferential cognition. Madhyamikas also seem to maintain that these ways of knowing are, in some sense, deceptive and therefore not ultimately valid. If that is so, the Samkhyas are saying, how can these deceptive cognitions ascertain even everyday objects that are said to exist? Wouldn't the objects too become false and unreal? And if this is so, the Samkhyas argue, doesn't that then mean that emptiness itself becomes unreal and meditation on emptiness useless?

The Madhyamika responds to this by accepting the consequence that, generally speaking, objects that are established by deceptive cognitions must also be unreal and false.

139. If there is no object for analysis,
There can be no grasping of its nonexistence.
Therefore, a deceptive object of whatever kind
Will also have an emptiness equally deceptive.

The Prasangika-Madhyamikas maintain that the valid cognition of emptiness—and indeed emptiness, too, in the final analysis—lacks absolute existence. So the Prasangika-Madhyamikas respond, "Yes, we agree, just as the cognition ascertaining emptiness is deceptive, similarly emptiness too is devoid of ultimate existence."

In relation to this verse, Minyak Künsö's commentary observes that there is no emptiness unrelated to or independent of an object. That is, the emptiness of a vase is necessarily associated with the vase. There can be no independently existing emptiness of the vase separate from the vase. So when the theory of emptiness is contemplated, we take an existing entity—be it an object or an event—and then use the argument of dependent origination to establish it. Because things and events exist only by dependence on other factors, they are empty of self, or intrinsic existence. Since the object is unreal and false and therefore not truly existent, the emptiness that is the quality or nature of that phenomenon will also ultimately be unreal and ultimately not truly existent.

In the next verse, Shantideva uses an analogy to further illustrate this point.

140. Thus, when in a dream, a child has died,
The state of mind that thinks he is no more
Will overwhelm the thought that he was living.
And yet, both thoughts are equally deceptive.

The analogy is that if you dream that your child dies, then in the dream you will think "Now my child no longer exists" and feel sorrow as a result. This very thought of your child's nonexistence prevents the thought of his existence arising. However, this too is false.

All things and events can be analyzed from both the conventional viewpoint and the absolute viewpoint, and so are said to have two natures, or two truths—conventional and ultimate truth. When we examine an object such as a vase and analyze whether it exists inherently or not, what we find is its emptiness. When we then take that emptiness as the object of our analysis and examine whether it too exists inherently or not, what we then find is the emptiness of emptiness. So even emptiness, when analyzed regarding the ultimate nature of its existence, is revealed to enjoy the same status as all other objects—it too has no intrinsic existence.

Typically, emptiness is taken as ultimate truth. However, when we take emptiness itself as the object of an ultimate analysis, emptiness becomes a conventional truth. Emptiness has, in some sense, "shifted its position," and we see that it too is devoid of intrinsic existence, and is thus, in this relative frame of reference, a conventional truth.

Shantideva concludes the diamond splinters argument:

141. Therefore, as we see through such investigation,
Nothing is that does not have a cause;
And nothing is existent in its causes
Taken one by one or in the aggregate.

142ab. It does not come from somewhere else,
Neither does it stay, nor yet depart.

At this point in his commentary, Minyak Künsö says of all things and events that "their ultimate nature is beyond notions of permanence and nihilism."

The Great Dependent Origination Argument

Next is the reasoning of dependent origination, which is said to be the *king of all reasoning* in establishing the emptiness of inherent existence. The reason for this epithet of the *king* or *chief* of all proofs is that all forms of logical argument establishing emptiness must, either directly or indirectly, be rooted in the idea of dependent origination. Using dependent origination as a logical basis to establish the emptiness of all things and events confers a unique advantage: through the applying this reasoning, we not only avoid the extreme of absolutism but also the extreme of nihilism.

So, in the following verses Shantideva explains that any thing or event that comes into being in dependence on its parts, causes and conditions, or conceptual designation is like a mirage, or a magic illusion—it is, in some sense, fabricated. Like the reflection of a form in a mirror, which arises naturally when an object is placed in front of it, all things and events are created through their dependence on many factors, as a result of the aggregation of many conditions.

142cd. How will what confusion takes for truth
In any sense be different from a mirage?

143. Things, then, bodied forth by magic spells,
And that which is displayed by dint of causes—
"Whence have these arisen?" we should ask;
And where they go to, that we should examine!

144. What arises through the meeting of conditions
And ceases to exist when these are lacking,
Is artificial like the mirror image;
How can true existence be ascribed to it?

So dependent origination can be understood at several different levels—dependence on causes and conditions, dependence on component parts, and dependence on conceptual designation, in other words labels and concepts.

The Tibetan term *tenjung* is a composite of two syllables meaning *dependently (ten)* and *originated (jung),* and this term implies a middle way that is free of the two extremes of permanence and nihilism. According to this implication, all things and events are understood to emerge by depending on other causes and conditions. This idea of *dependence* negates absolutism by demonstrating that things and events do not enjoy any independent status; that lack of autonomy precludes the possibility of substantial reality. *Origination,* however, implies existence and affirms the reality of the relative world, meaning that we can—even in the face of emptiness—sustain the validity of such notions as cause and effect, samsara and nirvana, and so on. So the very meaning of the term *dependent origination* suggests the negation of the extremes of both absolutism and nihilism.

The Argument in Terms of Existence and Nonexistence

Next is the argument concerning the origination and cessation of entities and nonentities. It is presented mainly from the point of view of the effect, or fruition.

145. Something that exists with true existence—
What need is there for it to have a cause?
Something that is wholly nonexistent—
Again, what need has it to have a cause?

146. Even by a hundred million causes,
No transformation is there in nonentity.
For if this keeps its status, how could entity occur?
And likewise, what is there that could so change?

147. When nonbeing prevails, if there's no being,
When could being ever supervene?
For insofar as entity does not occur,
Nonentity itself will not depart.

148. And if nonentity is not dispersed,
No chance is there for entity to manifest.
Being cannot change and turn to nonbeing,
Otherwise it has a double nature.

149. Thus there is no being,
Likewise no cessation.
Therefore beings, each and every one,
Are unborn and are never ceasing.

If things exist independently, enjoying a discrete and intrinsic existence, what need is there for a cause? If things exist inherently, truly, and autonomously, then a cause will have no role to play, because the role of causes is to bring effects into being.

Having thus negated intrinsic origination and cessation, the conclusion arrived at is that processes such as origination and cessation can be understood only in terms of mere conditionality. When understood in this way, we are able to see the fundamental equality of samsara and nirvana. This is because, from the perspective of their emptiness of intrinsic existence, there is no difference whatsoever between samsara and nirvana.

Shantideva concludes this argument with the following statement:

150. Wandering beings, thus, resemble dreams
And also the banana tree, if you examine well.
No difference is there, in their own true nature,
Between the states of suffering and beyond-all-sorrow.

Aspiring to Realize the Wisdom of Emptiness

Shantideva now concludes the wisdom chapter by describing the benefits of contemplating emptiness. He says that understanding emptiness will firstly ensure that we do not become enslaved by mundane concerns; in fact, we will be able to trample upon worldly conventions. Secondly, we enhance our potential for compassion by training our mind in this wisdom. Shantideva lists these as the two principal benefits of meditating on emptiness.

151. Thus, with things devoid of true existence,
What is there to gain, and what to lose?
Who is there to pay me court and honors,
And who is there to scorn and to revile me?

152. Pain and pleasure, whence do these arise?
And what is there to give me joy and sorrow?
In this quest and search for perfect truth,
Who is craving, what is there to crave?

153. Examine now this world of living beings:
Who is there therein to pass away?
What is there to come, and what has been?
And who, indeed, are relatives and friends?

154. May beings like myself discern and grasp
That all things have the character of space![18]
But those who long for happiness and ease,
Through disputes or the cause of pleasures,

155. Are deeply troubled, or else thrilled with joy.
They suffer, strive, contend among themselves,
Slashing, stabbing, injuring each other:
They live their lives engulfed in many evils.

156. From time to time they surface in the states of bliss,
Abandoning themselves to many pleasures.
But dying, down they fall to suffer torment,
Long, unbearable, in realms of sorrow.

157. Many are the chasms and abysses of existence,
Where the truth of emptiness is not found.
All is contradiction, all denial,
Suchness,[19] or its like, can find no place.

158. There, exceeding all description,
Is the shoreless sea of pain unbearable.
Here it is that strength is low,
And lives are flickering and brief.

159. All activities for sake of life and health,
Relief of hunger and of weariness,
Time consumed in sleep, all accident and injury,
And sterile friendships with the childish—

160. Thus life passes quickly, meaningless.
True discernment—hard it is to have!
How then shall we ever find the means
To curb the futile wanderings of the mind?

161. Further, evil forces work and strain
To cast us headlong into states of woe;
Manifold are false, deceptive trails,
And it is hard to dissipate our doubts.

162. Hard it is to find again this state of freedom,
Harder yet to come upon enlightened teachers,
Hard, indeed, to turn aside the torrent of
defilement!
Alas, our sorrows fall in endless streams!

163. Sad it is indeed that living beings,
Carried on the flood of bitter pain,
However terrible their plight may be,
Do not perceive they suffer so!

164. Some there are who bathe themselves repeatedly,
And afterward they scorch themselves with fire,
Suffering intensely all the while,
Yet there they stay, proclaiming loud their bliss.

165. Likewise there are some who live and act
As though old age and death will never come
to them.
But then life's over, and there comes
The dreadful fall into the states of loss.

166. When shall I be able to allay and quench
The dreadful heat of suffering's blazing fires,
With plenteous rains of my own bliss
That pour torrential from my clouds of merit?

167. My wealth of merit gathered in,
With reverence but without conceptual aim,
When shall I reveal this truth of emptiness
To those who go to ruin through belief in substance?

With this, a brief exposition of the ninth chapter of Shantideva's *The Way of the Bodhisattva* is completed.

MEDITATION

Let us meditate now on perceiving all sentient beings as having an illusion-like nature, as explained in the conclusion of Shantideva's ninth chapter. We can observe the futility of generating strong fluctuating emotional states, such as anger and jealousy, toward others. Although sentient beings are like illusions, they also feel pain and joy. Reflect upon the empty nature of self and others, and try to overcome the forces of these negative tendencies, the afflictive emotions such as anger and desire. Then reflect that all sentient beings possess the potential for freedom from suffering, and with that awareness, generate strong compassion toward all sentient beings. Let us try to meditate, for about five minutes, by cultivating such compassion.

12. GENERATING THE AWAKENING MIND

PRACTICING WISDOM

The Benefits of Cherishing Others

Shantideva states that all happiness and joy are the consequences of cherishing the well-being of other sentient beings, while all problems, tragedies, and disasters are the consequences of self-cherishing attitudes. What further need is there, he asks, to talk about this when we can see the qualities of the Buddha, who cherishes the welfare of other sentient beings, and the fate of ourselves, who are in this current state? We can easily be convinced of this by comparing the shortcomings of ordinary sentient beings with the enlightened qualities and wisdom of the buddhas. On the basis of this comparison, we are able to see the benefits and merits of the aspiration to cherish the welfare of other sentient beings and the faults and disadvantages of a self-cherishing and self-centered attitude.

Shantideva asks, since self and others are equal in having the innate desire to be happy and to overcome suffering, why do we seek our own self-interest at the expense of others—even to the extent of being totally oblivious to them? I think this points to something very true. Like oneself, all other sentient beings are equal in having this wish to be happy and to overcome suffering.

Each of us individually is not satisfied with any level of joy and happiness, and this is true of all sentient beings. Just as I, as an individual, have the natural right to fulfill this basic aspiration, so do all other sentient beings. It is crucial to recognize this fundamental equality.

What then is the difference between self and others? No matter how important and precious each person is, we are only talking about the well-being of one person. No matter how acute their suffering may be, we are still concerned here with the interest of one single person. In contrast, when we speak about the well-being of other sentient beings, this word *other* refers to limitless, countless sentient beings. In the case of this *other,* even if we are dealing with slight degrees of suffering, when aggregated, we are talking about the sufferings of an infinite number of beings. Therefore, from the point of view of quantity, the welfare of other sentient beings becomes far more important than that of oneself.

Even from the point of view of our own self-interest, if others are happy and satisfied, then we ourselves can also be happy. On the other hand, if others are in a perpetual state of suffering, then we too will suffer from the same fate. The interest of others is intimately linked with our own self-interest; this is very true. Furthermore, based on our own personal experience, we can observe that the more we hold onto a strong sense of self—cherishing our own self-interest—the greater our own emotional and psychological problems.

Of course the pursuit of our own self-interest is very important. However, we need a more realistic approach, that is, not to take self-interest too seriously but spend more time thinking about the well-being of other sentient beings. Being more altruistic and taking into account the feelings and well-being of other sentient beings is, in actual fact, a much more healthy approach in pursuing our own interests. If we do that, we will see a marked change, a feeling of relaxation. We will no longer be easily provoked by petty circumstances, thinking that everything is at stake, and acting as if our whole image, identity, and existence is being threatened. On the other hand, if we constantly think of our own self-interest—totally oblivious to the well-being of other sentient beings—then even the tiniest circumstances can provoke deep feelings of hurt and disturbance. The truth of this is something we can judge from our own experience.

In the long run, generating a good heart will benefit both ourselves and others. In contrast, allowing our minds to remain enslaved by self-centeredness will only perpetuate our feelings of dissatisfaction, frustration, and unhappiness, both in temporary terms and in the long term as well. We will waste this wonderful opportunity we have now—of being born as a human, of being equipped with this wonderful human faculty of intelligence, which can be utilized for higher purposes. So it is important to be able to weigh these long-term and short-term consequences. What better way to make our human existence meaningful than by meditating on bodhichitta—the altruistic aspiration to attain enlightenment for the sake of all sentient beings.

Generating the Awakening Mind

On my part, I cannot claim to have realized the awakening mind or bodhichitta. However, I have a deep admiration for bodhichitta. I feel that the admiration I have for bodhichitta is my wealth and a source of my courage. This is also the basis of my happiness; it is what enables me to make others happy, and it is the factor that makes me feel satisfied and content. I am thoroughly dedicated and committed to this altruistic ideal. Whether sick or well, growing old, or even at the point of death, I shall remain committed to this ideal. I am convinced that I will always maintain my deep admiration for this ideal of generating the altruistic mind of bodhichitta. On your part too, my friends, I would like to appeal to you to try to become as familiar as possible with bodhichitta. Strive, if you can, to generate such an altruistic and compassionate state of mind.

Actual realization of bodhichitta requires years of meditative practice. In some cases, it may take eons to have this realization. It is not adequate simply to have an intellectual understanding of what bodhichitta is. Nor is it sufficient to have an intuitive feeling like, "May all sentient beings attain the fully enlightened state." These are not a realization of bodhichitta. Even so, I think it is worth it, for what more profound practice of Dharma is there? As Shantideva states:

1:10. For like the supreme substance of the alchemists,
It takes the impure form of human flesh
And makes of it the priceless body of a buddha.
Such is bodhichitta: we should grasp it firmly!

When we think of bodhichitta superficially, it may seem quite simple; it may not even appear all that compelling. In contrast, the tantric meditations on mandalas and deities might seem mysterious, and we may find them more appealing. However, when we actually engage in the practice, bodhichitta is inexhaustible. There is also no danger of becoming disillusioned or disheartened as a result of practicing bodhichitta, whereas in meditations on deity yoga, reciting mantras, and so on, there is a danger of becoming disillusioned, because we often enter into such practices with too high an expectation. After many years, we might think, "Although I have done deity yoga meditation and recited all these mantras, there is no noticeable change; I haven't had any mystical experiences." This type of disillusionment is not the case with the practice of bodhichitta.

Since the realization of bodhichitta requires a long period of practice, once you have slight experience, it is vital that you affirm your cultivation of bodhichitta through aspirational prayers. This can be done in the presence of a guru or in the presence of a representation of a buddha. Such a practice can further enhance your capacity for generating bodhichitta. By taking the bodhisattva vow in a special ceremony, you affirm your generation of bodhichitta in the presence of a teacher.

The first part of this type of ceremony is the generation of aspirational bodhichitta. What is involved here is that by generating this altruistic aspiration to attain buddhahood for the benefit of all beings, you pledge that you will not give it up or let it degenerate, not only in this lifetime, but also in future lives. As a commitment, there are certain precepts to be observed. The second part is the ceremony for taking the bodhisattva vows. This should be done by someone who has already prepared themselves by going through the first stage.

Having developed enthusiasm for engaging in the bodhisattva's deeds, you then take the bodhisattva vows. Once you have taken bodhisattva vows, whether you like it or not, whether it is pleasurable or not, what is required as a commitment is to keep the vows as precious as your own life. To make that pledge, you must have determination as solid as a mountain; you are making a pledge that from now on you will follow the precepts of the bodhisattva and lead your life according to the bodhisattva training.

Of course some readers are not practicing Buddhists, and even among practicing Buddhists, some may not feel committed to taking the bodhisattva vows, especially the second part.[20] If you feel hesitant about being able to observe the bodhisattva vows, then it is best not to make the pledge; you can still generate an altruistic mind and wish that all sentient beings may be happy and pray that you may be able to attain full enlightenment for the sake of all sentient beings. This should be sufficient; you will gain the merit of generating bodhichitta, but you do not have to follow the precepts. Also, there is less danger of breaking the vows. So if you do not take any vows, you simply develop aspirational bodhichitta. You can be your own judge.

> With the wish to free all beings
> I shall always go for refuge
> To the Buddha, Dharma, and Sangha
> Until I reach full enlightenment.

Enthused by wisdom and compassion,
Today in the Buddha's presence
I generate the mind for full awakening
For the benefit of all sentient beings.

As long as space remains,
As long as sentient beings remain,
Until then, may I too remain
and dispel the miseries of the world.

NOTES

1. A complete English translation of this work from the Sanskrit original can be found in Carol Meadows's *Ārya-śura's Compendium of the Perfections* (Bonn: Indica et Tibetetica Verlag, 1986).
2. An authoritative English translation of this important Buddhist classic by John Dunne and Sara McClintock was published as *The Precious Garland: An Epistle to a King* (Boston: Wisdom Publications, 1997). This limited-edition publication was prepared for the commentary given by the Dalai Lama on the text in Los Angeles that year. A revised edition of Dunne and McClintock's translation is forthcoming from Wisdom along with a new translation of Nagarjuna's *Mulamadhyamakakarika.*
3. Only partial translation of this work exists in European languages.
4. See, for instance, *Transcendent Wisdom: A Commentary on the Ninth Chapter of Shantideva's Guide to the Bodhisattva Way of Life,* trans. and ed. by B. Alan Wallace (Ithaca NY: Snow Lion Publications, 1988).
5. An English translation of the section on the ninth chapter from both of these two Tibetan commentaries was produced by the Padmakara Translation Group and published by Editions Padmakara in 1993 under the title of *Wisdom: Two Buddhist Commentaries.* Minyak Künsö is also known as Thupten Chökyi Drakpa.
6. These were published as *A Flash of Lightning in the Dark of Night: A Guide to the Bodhisattva's Way of Life,* trans. by the Padmakara Translation Group (Boston: Shambhala Publications, 1994).

7. *Sutra Presenting the First [Link in the Chain of] Dependent Origination and Its Divisions.* Toh 211, Kangyur, *mdo sde,* vol. *tsha,* 123b.
8. "First avert what is not meritorious / In the middle avert [grasping at] self / Finally, dismantle all views and avert them / Whoever knows this is indeed wise." ch. 8, v. 5. For an alternative English translation of this stanza with commentary, see *Yogic Deeds of Bodhisattvas: Gyel-tsap on Aryadeva's Four Hundred,* commentary by Geshe Sönam Rinchen, trans. and ed. by Ruth Sönam (Ithaca NY: Snow Lion Publications, 1994), p. 193.
9. A clear presentation of Tsongkhapa's reading of this important line can be found in *Notes on the Wisdom Chapter,* The Collected Works of Tsongkhapa, vol. 14.
10. For an extended commentary by His Holiness on this central Buddhist text, see *Essence of the Heart Sutra* (Boston: Wisdom Publications, 2002).
11. A proponent of the Madhyamaka school is a Madhyamika.
12. This is most probably a reference to the following stanza: "So when the yogis / Have developed this emptiness [in their minds], / No doubt that the altruistic thoughts / Concerned with other's welfare will arise." *Bodhichittavivarana,* v. 73.
13. For the Dalai Lama's own commentary on this practice, see *Kalachakra Tantra: Rite of Initiation,* trans. and introduced by Jeffrey Hopkins (Boston: Wisdom Publications, 1999).
14. Ch. 1, v. 80; for an English translation of this verse, see *The Precious Garland,* trans. by John Dunne and Sara McClintock (Boston: Wisdom Publications, 1997), p. 21.
15. This analysis is found in ch. 22 of Nagarjuna's *Stanzas on the Fundamental Wisdom of the Middle Way.*
16. *The Precious Garland,* ch. 2, v. 73d–74. For an English translation of these lines, see John Dunne et al., p. 36.
17. Ch. 24, v. 19.
18. Khenpo Künpal, in his commentary, says all things are like space because they elude the conceptual categories of "is" and "is not."
19. The way things really are, or the nature of reality itself.
20. The actual rite for taking the bodhisattva vows is not included in this book.

BIBLIOGRAPHY OF TEXTS CITED

Sutras

Dependent Origination Sutra (Pratityasamutpada adivibhanga nirdesha sutra). (Tib. *rten cing 'brel bar 'byung ba dang po dang rnam par dbye ba bstan pa;* Toh 211, Kangyur, *mdo sde,* vol. *tsha,* 123b–125a).

Heart Sutra (Prajnaparamita Hridaya Sutra). (Tib. *shes rab kyi pha rol du phyin pa'i snying po;* Toh 21, Kangyur, *shes phyin,* vol. *ka,* 144b–146a).

Indian Treatises

Aryadeva. *Four Hundred Verses (Chatushatakashastra)*. (Tib. *rnal 'byor spyod pa bzhi brgya pa;* Toh 3846, Tengyur, *dbu ma,* vol. *tsha,* 1b–18a). Complete English translation of this work with extant fragments of the Sanskrit original can be found in Karen Lang's *Āryadeva's Catuḥśataka* (Copenhagen: Akademisk Forlag, 1986). A translation of the root stanzas from the Tibetan edition with Gyaltsap Je's commentary can be found under the title *The Yogic Deeds of Bodhisattva: Gyel-tsap on Aryadeva's Four Hundred* (Ithaca: Snow Lion, 1994), translated and edited by Ruth Sönam.

Aryashura. *Compendium of the Perfections (Paramitasamasa)*. (Tib. *pha rol du phyin pa bsdus pa;* Toh 3944, Tengyur, *dbu ma,* vol. *khi,* 217b–235a). Complete English translation of this work from the

Sanskrit original can be found in Carol Meadows's *Ārya-śura's Compendium of the Perfections* (Bonn: Indica et Tibetetica Verlag, 1986).

Asanga. *Bodhisattva Levels (Bodhisattvabhumi)*. (Tib. *rnal 'byor spyod pa'i sa las byang chub sems pa'i sa;* Toh 4037, Tengyur, *sems tsam,* vol. *vi,* 1b–213a).

———. *Compendium of Higher Knowledge (Abhidharmasamuchaya)*. (Tib. *chos mngo pa kun las btus pa;* Toh 4049, Tengyur, *sems tsam,* vol. *ri,* 1b–77a, 44b–120a). English translation of this work from Walpola Rahula's French translation undertaken by Sara Boin-Webb in *Abhidharmasamuccaya: The Compendium of the Higher Teaching* (Fremont: Asian Humanities Press, 2001).

———. *The Sublime Continuum (Uttaratantra)*. (Tib. *theg pa chen po rgyud bla ma;* Toh 4024, Tengyur, *sems tsam,* vol. *phi,* 54b–73a). English translation of this work can be found under the title *The Changeless Nature* (Eskdalemuir, Scotland: Karma Drubgyud Dharjay Ling, 1985), translated by Ken and Katia Holmes.

Bhavaviveka. *Blaze of Reasoning (Tarkajvala)*. (Tib. *dbu ma rtog ge 'bar ba;* Toh 3856, Tengyur, *dbu ma,* vol. *dza,* 40b–329b).

Chandrakirti. *Clear Words: Commentary on the "Fundamental Wisdom of the Middle Way" (Prasannapada)*. (Tib. *dbu ma rtsa ba'i 'grel pa tshig gsal ba;* Toh 3860, Tengyur, *dbu ma,* vol. *ha,* 1b–200a).

———. *Commentary on "Four Hundred Verses on the Middle Way" (Chatushatakatika)*. (Tib. *bzhi brgya pa'i rgya cher 'grel pa;* Toh 3865, Tengyur, *dbu ma,* vol. *ya,* 30b–239a).

———. *Supplement to the Middle Way (Madhyamakavatara)*. (Tib. *dbu ma la 'jug pa;* Toh 3861, Tengyur, *dbu ma,* vol. *ha,* 201b–219a). An English translation of this work can be found in C.W. Huntington, Jr.'s *The Emptiness of Emptiness* (Honolulu: University of Hawaii, 1989).

Dharmakirti. *Commentary on the "Valid Cognition" (Pramanavarttika)*. (Tib. *tshad ma rnam 'grel gyi tshig le'ur byas pa;* Toh 4210, Tengyur, *tshad ma,* vol. *ce,* 94b–151a).

Nagarjuna. *Commentary on the Awakening Mind (Bodhichittavivarana).* (Tib. *byang chup sems kyi 'grel pa;* Toh 1800 and 1801, Tengyur, *rgyud,* vol. *ngi,* 38a–42b, 42b–45a). An English translation of this short work can be found in Chr. Lindtner's *Nagarjuniana: Studies in the Writings and Philosophy of Nāgārjuna* (Delhi: Motilal Banarsidass, 1987).

———. *Compendium of Sutras (Sutrasamuchaya).* (Tib. *mdo kun las btus pa;* Toh 3934, Tengyur, *dbu ma,* vol. *ki,* 148b–215a).

———. *The Precious Garland (Ratnavali).* (Tib. *rgyal po la gtam bya ba rin po che'i phreng ba;* Toh 4158, Tengyur, *spring yig,* vol. *ge,* 107a–126a). An English translation of this work by John Dunne and Sara McClintock exists under the title *The Precious Garland: An Epistle to a King* (Boston: Wisdom Publications, 1997).

———. *Stanzas on the Fundamental Wisdom of the Middle Way (Mulamadhyamakakarika).* (Tib. *dbu ma rtsa ba'i tshig le'ur byas pa;* Toh 3824, Tengyur, *dbu ma,* vol. *tsa,* 1b–19a). There are numerous English translations of this work, including Fredrick Streng's *Emptiness: A Study in Meaning* (Nashville: Abington Press, 1967), Kenneth Inada's *Nāgārjuna: A Translation of His Mulamādhyamakakārika with an Introductory Essay* (Tokyo: The Hokuseido Press, 1970), and Jay Garfield's *The Fundamental Wisdom of the Middle Way* (New York: Oxford University Press, 1995).

Prajnakaramati. *Explanation of the Difficult Points of "Guide to the Bodhisattva's Way of Life" (Bodhicaryavatarapanjika).* (Tib. *byang chub sems pa'i spyod pa la 'jug pa'i dka' 'grel;* Toh 3873, Tengyur, *dbu ma,* vol. *la,* 288b–349a).

Shantarakshita. *Ornament of the Middle Way (Madhyamakalamkara).* (Tib. *dbu ma rgyan gyi tshig le'ur byas pa;* Toh 3884, Tengyur, *dbu ma,* vol. *sa,* 53a–56b).

Shantideva. *Compendium of Deeds (Shikshasamuchaya).* (Tib. *bslab pa kun las btus pa;* Toh 3940, Tengyur, *dbu ma,* vol. *khi,* 3a–194b). Translated into English from Sanskrit by Cecil Bendall and W.H.D. Rouse (Delhi: Motilal Banarsidass, 1971; reprinted).

———. *The Way of the Bodhisattva (Bodhicharyavatara)*. (Tib. *byang chup sems pa'i spyod pa la 'jug pa;* Toh 3871, Tengyur, *dbu ma,* vol. *la,* 1b–40a). Several English translations of this work exist, including Stephen Batchelor's *Guide to the Bodhisattva's Way of Life* (Dharamsala: Library of Tibetan Works & Archives, 1979), *The Way of the Bodhisattva,* translated by the Padmakara Translation Group (Boston: Shambhala Publications, 1997), as well as *The Bodhicaryāvatāra,* translated by Kate Krosby and Andrew Skilton (New York: Oxford University Press, 1995).

Vasubandhu. *Treasury of Higher Knowledge (Abhidharmakosha)*. (Tib. *chos mngo pa mdzod kyi tshig le'ur byas pa;* Toh 4089, Tengyur, *mngon pa,* vol. *ku,* 1b–25a). English translation from La Valleé Poussin's French edition found in Leo M. Pruden, *Abhidharmakośa-bhāṣyam* (Fremont: Asian Humanities Press, 1991).

Tibetan Works

Künsang Palden, Khenpo. *Sacred Words of My Teacher Manjushri (byang chub sems dpa'i spyod pa la 'jug pa rtsa ba dang 'grel pa)*. Typeset edition (Sichuan: National Minorities Press, 1990).

Künsang Sönam, Minyak. *Brilliant Lamp Illuminating the Suchness of Profound Dependent Origination (spyod 'jug gi 'grel bshad rgyal sras yon tan bum bzang)*. Typeset edition (Xinhua: National Minorities Press, 1990).

Mipham Jamyang Namgyal Gyatso. *Exposition of the Ornament of the Middle Way (dbu ma rgyan gyi rnam bshad)*. The Collected Works of Ju Mipham, vol. *nga* (4).

Tsongkhapa. *Notes on the Wisdom Chapter.* The Collected Works of Tsongkhapa, vol. *pha* (14).

Gyaltsap Je. *Gateway of Entrance for the Bodhisattvas: A Thorough Exposition of the Guide to the Bodhisattva's Way of Life (byang chub sems dpa'i spyod pa la 'jug pa'i rnam bshad rgyal sras 'jug ngogs)*. The Collected Works of Gyaltsap Je, vol. *nga* (4).

INDEX

Essence of the Heart Sutra: The Dalai Lama's Heart of Wisdom Teachings
Tenzin Gyatso, the 14th Dalai Lama
192 pages, ISBN 0-86171-318-4, $22.95

This is the best available resource for studying and understanding one of Buddhism's seminal and best-known texts, the *Heart Sutra*. Masterfully translated and edited by Geshe Thupten Jinpa, this volume comprises the Dalai Lama's famous Heart of Wisdom teachings of 2001, including an overview of Buddhism, background material, as well as commentary on the text.

The World of Tibetan Buddhism: An Overview of Its Philosophy and Practice
Tenzin Gyatso, the 14th Dalai Lama
224 pages, ISBN 0-86171-097-5, $15.95

"The definitive book on Tibetan Buddhism by the world's ultimate authority."
—*The Reader's Review*

The Compassionate Life
Tenzin Gyatso, the 14th Dalai Lama
128 pages, ISBN 0-86171-378-8, $11.95

"It is all here, everything we need to enact in our own lives, even in the most trying of times, if we are to realize the possibilities of true happiness in this very life. A sorely-needed prescription for sanity and kindness in the world."—Jon Kabat-Zinn, author of *Wherever You Go, There You Are*

Introduction to Tantra: The Transformation of Desire
Lama Yeshe
Introduction by Jonathan Landaw
Foreword by Philip Glass
192 pages, ISBN 0-86171-162-9, $16.95

"The best introductory work on Tibetan Buddhist tantra available, readily accessible to Western students."—Professor Janet Gyatso, Hershey Chair of Buddhist Studies, Harvard University

Becoming the Compassion Buddha: Tantric Mahamudra for Everyday Life
Lama Yeshe
Edited by Robina Courtin
Foreword by Geshe Lhundub Sopa
224 pages, ISBN 0-86171-343-5, $14.95

Lama Yeshe provides a commentary on a short guru yoga practice written by His Holiness the Fourteenth Dalai Lama. The practice includes visualizations that inspire the development of compassion and wisdom. The final section of the book goes into detail on the subject of Mahamudra, a meditation on the true nature of all phenomena—a potentially tricky subject. Here again, Lama Yeshe presents the teachings by drawing on examples from daily life and by introducing meditation practices that all can follow.

The Bliss of Inner Fire: Heart Practice of the Six Yogas of Naropa
Lama Yeshe
Foreword by Lama Zopa Rinpoche
224 pages, ISBN 0-86171-136-X, $16.95

"In a sense, *The Bliss of Inner Fire* is like a second *Introduction to Tantra*, opening up the world of Highest Yoga Tantra's advanced practices the way the earlier work opened up the world of tantra in general."—from the introduction by Jonathan Landaw

WISDOM PUBLICATIONS

Wisdom Publications, a nonprofit publisher, is dedicated to making available authentic Buddhist works for the benefit of all. We publish translations of the sutras and tantras, commentaries and teachings of past and contemporary Buddhist masters, and original works by the world's leading Buddhist scholars. We publish our titles with the appreciation of Buddhism as a living philosophy and with the special commitment to preserve and transmit important works from all the major Buddhist traditions.

To learn more about Wisdom, or to browse books online, visit our website at wisdompubs.org. You may request a copy of our mail-order catalog online or by writing to:

Wisdom Publications
199 Elm Street
Somerville, Massachusetts 02144 USA
Telephone: 617-776-7416
Fax: 617-776-7841
Email: info@wisdompubs.org
www.wisdompubs.org

THE WISDOM TRUST

As a nonprofit publisher, Wisdom is dedicated to the publication of fine Dharma books for the benefit of all sentient beings and dependent upon the kindness and generosity of sponsors in order to do so. If you would like to make a donation to Wisdom, please do so through our Somerville office. If you would like to sponsor the publication of a book, please write or email us at the address above.
Thank you.

Wisdom is a nonprofit, charitable 501(c)(3) organization affiliated with the Foundation for the Preservation of the Mahayana Tradition (FPMT).